UNDER ATTACK, FIGHTING BACK

UNDER ATTACK, FIGHTING BACK

Women and Welfare in the United States

MIMI ABRAMOVITZ

MONTHLY REVIEW PRESS
NEW YORK

Library of Congress Cataloging-in-Publication Data

Abramovitz, Mimi.
  Under attack, fighting back : women and welfare in the United States / Mimi
Abramovitz.
    p.   cm. — (Cornerstone books)
  Includes index.
  ISBN 0-85345-963-0 (paper). — ISBN 0-85345-962-2 (cloth : alk. paper)
    1. Welfare recipients—United States. 2. Poor women—United States. 3. Aid to
families with dependent children programs—United States. 4. Public welfare—
United States. 5. Welfare rights movement—United States. I. Title. II. Series:
Cornerstone books (New York, N.Y.)
HV91.A27 1995
362.83'086942—dc20   94-339990
                                                                          CIP

Monthly Review Press
122 West 27th Street
New York, NY 10001

Manufactured in the United States of America
10 9 8 7 6 5 4 3 2 1

CONTENTS

ACKNOWLEDGMENTS

This book reflects my experiences as a welfare worker, college teacher, researcher, and social activist, and my participation in the antiwar, civil rights, and women's movements. But most of all, I have been influenced by the welfare rights movement which I was fortunate to work with in the 1960s and again today. I titled this book *Under Attack, Fighting Back,* after a national conference that I attended in 1992 organized by women on welfare in Oakland, California. It is to past, current, and future welfare mothers that this book is dedicated.

The process of creating a book depends on the support of others. I am indebted to the many feminist scholars who share my interest in women and the welfare state and who have persistently pursued this research. Martha Davis, Linda Gordon, Roberta Spalter-Roth, Rickie Solinger, and Guida West provided useful comments on an early draft of the book, although they in no way are responsible for my opinions or errors. Books like this could not be written without the work of the Center on Social Welfare Law and Policy, the Center for Law and Social Welfare Policy, the Center on Budget and Policy Priorities, and other advocacy groups who tracked legislative developments that many of us outside of the nation's capital could not follow on our own.

I am also grateful to the Hunter College Center for the Study of Family Policy for its commitment to low-income women. The leadership provided by its director, Janet Poppendeick, herself a scholar and activist; the Center's support for the Welfare Rights Initiative which, led by Melinda Lackey, trains college students on public assistance to become community leaders and organizers; and the uplift I experience from my work with the students themselves, made an enormous difference to me as I struggled with this book. I also drew sustenance from working with the Welfare Reform Task Force of the New York City chapter of the National Association of Social Workers; the Bertha Capen Reynolds Society, the national organization of progressive social workers; the New York City Welfare Reform Network; and the Committee of One Hundred Women, which brought the voice of middle-class women into the welfare struggle. The hard work of all these people belies the idea that advocacy is dead.

But this book would not have seen the light of day without the patient, careful, skillful editing work of Susan Lowes, the unflappable director of Monthly Review Press, and Akiko Ichikawa, her assistant, also put in endless hours on editing, selecting graphics, and dealing with my many questions with utmost patience. My family and friends, but especially my husband, Bob Abramovitz, were extraordinarily supportive as I immersed myself in my cluttered study. Bob trusted my ideas, read and reread chapters, and provided important intellectual insights and correctives. Perhaps most importantly, he made sure that I relaxed, went to the movies, hiked in the woods, and ate good food. And he was there—always—when I needed him.

PREFACE

Politicians and policymakers regularly declare that the welfare system is broken and needs to be fixed, and that the wider public supports scrapping the program that serves single mothers and their children. However, life is not that simple. Despite negative attitudes toward the government's performance, there is considerable sentiment in favor of public spending for the poor. One major national poll concluded:

> An overwhelming majority believes that society is morally obliged to try to eliminate poverty and that such efforts are a good economic investment. Support for fighting poverty does not seem to be any weaker than it was during the 1960s War on Poverty, and may be stronger.

The polls also reveal that the responses of the voters depend on how the question is framed. A national survey conducted during 1994 asked, "Do you think Government spending on welfare should be increased, decreased, or kept about the same?" Nearly half of the respondents favored a decrease. But when the question was asked using the phrase "programs for the poor" instead of "welfare," the sentiment was reversed: nearly half favored more spending.

Two other surveys found that large numbers of Americans want to see the welfare system fixed without punishing the recipients or their children. While the public strongly endorses programs that move people into productive work, it expresses "virtually no support for simply eliminating welfare and little support for cutting spending on it." Moreover, the polls approve of government intervention: "There is very strong support for job training and large-scale jobs programs, not only for current welfare recipients but for all able-bodied Americans willing to work." Those polled also believe that any welfare-to-work program should be accompanied by government-subsidized childcare, health insurance, transportation, and a job at the end of a time limit, including public service employment.

Feelings about family issues are more ambivalent but nonetheless sympathetic. While opposing policies that harm children, the public seems of two minds about ending benefits for women who have more kids while on welfare. In one poll, two-thirds of respondents approved of such a proposal, but 70 percent opposed it when the question included the phrase, "even if this would create hardship for the woman and her child."

Such polls highlight two important features of the current welfare reform debate: the powerfully negative impact of the word "welfare" on public attitudes toward government programs, and the failure of politicians to mobilize the wellspring of good will toward the poor found among people in the United States. The misperceptions about welfare stem from the stereotyping of poor women and welfare; the systematic refusal of the media to cover the ongoing resistance to harsh welfare reforms that have been organized by welfare mothers and their supporters around the country, and the bankrupt leadership of politicians who insist on playing to the worst instincts of the voters.

These realities cry out for a broader discussion of ways to improve welfare and to reduce, if not eliminate, poverty. My hope is that this book will help fill this need by offering an alternative perspective on the contemporary debates about welfare in the legislature, in the academy, and in the streets. Parts 1 and 2 of the book examine the myths and stereotypes that have fueled the current assault on welfare; explore the history of earlier attacks which, like the current one, targeted women's work and family life. They suggest that, in their repeated efforts to retrench public assistance, the nation's leaders have been responding to the fears of employers (that welfare undercuts wages) *and* to the fears of family-values advocates (that assistance to single mothers seriously challenges the patriarchal status quo). The history shows that poor women and public assistance have been scapegoated regularly to enforce both the work and family ethic; to ease public concerns about other social, economic, and political issues; and to divert public attention from the true causes of the nation's woes.

Part 3 moves us from the legislature into the academy, where explanations of social phenomena are developed in the first place. Despite the fact that public assistance and many other social welfare programs aid individuals through their families, the early literature on the welfare state rarely included women. For at least the past fifteen years, women in the academy have worked to change this. Women, after all, represent 50 percent of the population and the majority of welfare clients and workers, and the family, and thus the functioning of the wider social order, depends heavily on women's work in the home—work that is underwritten by the welfare state. The academy rarely welcomed and only reluctantly acknowledged this feminist scholarship. Nonetheless, women scholars fought back, and, by bringing women into view, transformed our knowledge of the welfare state.

Part 4 takes us into "the streets," where the power of capital and the state has been contested throughout the twentieth century and where, contrary to popular wisdom, women have always been active. From the black and white middle-class women reformers at the turn of the century to the militant housewives during the Depression to the welfare mothers of today, women have provided much of the leadership, and the legwork. First they insisted that merchants and landlords keep food, clothing, and shelter affordable so that women can carry out their caretaking work in the home. Then women turned their demands to the state, as it gradually began to cover some of these basic needs. When social programs came under attack, women mobilized again to defend them from the budget ax.

Social programs have always been a double-edged sword for women, regulating their lives on the one hand and providing needed resources on the other. The welfare state has always been an arena of political struggle for women. My wish in detailing this still incomplete history is threefold: to give visibility to the long neglected efforts of women to produce a better life for themselves and their families; to help empower current welfare rights activists by emphasizing what is known about their foremothers; and to stress the importance to social change of political pressure from below.

Although the fate of pending legislative proposals to overhaul welfare was not known when this book went to press in March 1996, all the signs indicated that Congress was about to pass a bill that would further restrict women's access to welfare. At the same time, women activists—poor, working, and middle-class; white, Latina, Asian, and African-American—were engaged in a struggle to defend welfare and to define it as an issue for all women. That women from different races and classes may conclude, sooner rather than later, that "an injury to one is an injury to all" has buoyed my spirits even as the nation's leaders move—ever so cruelly—to dismantle the welfare state. I remain hopeful that we will be able to defy the conflicts of race and class that have kept us apart in the past and enable us—with men—to continue the fight for a society based on equality and justice for all.

PART 1

UNDER ATTACK: WOMEN AND WELFARE REFORM TODAY

It's time to honor and reward people who work hard and play by the rules. That means ending welfare as we know it—not by punishing the poor or preaching to them, but by empowering Americans to take care of their children and improve their lives. No one who works full-time and has children at home should be poor anymore. No one who can work should be able to stay on welfare forever. —Bill Clinton, 1992[1]

I would rather be on welfare and have a place to live and a way to feed my children. I'll do what I have to do for my children to make sure that their well-being is taken care of. I am proud that I can take care of my children. —A welfare recipient, 1994[2]

Welfare reform has become a hot political issue. During his 1992 presidential election campaign, Bill Clinton drew loud and frequent applause when he declared that welfare should provide "a second chance, not a way of life." But by late 1994, his talk of work and responsibility had been upstaged by the Republicans' Personal Responsibility Act, which was part of the Contract With America and called for ending welfare altogether. By late 1995, both houses of Congress had passed bills that transformed Clinton's plan to move women off public assistance into one that increased the government's intervention in women's work and family lives and ended the sixty-year-old federal guarantee of aid for poor children and their families. Clinton's drive to reform welfare also opened the door to mean-spirited state reforms and weakened a long-standing taboo against cutting both Medicare and Social Security. Welfare reform became so harsh and punitive that welfare rights advocates launched a nationwide Veto Campaign. Clinton vetoed the first bill and may veto the second, but in the current political climate whatever legislation the President and Congress finally agree on is likely to be extremely regressive.

The debate over welfare is taking place in legislatures, on university campuses, and in the streets. In the pages that follow, we will be looking at the issues from a number of perspectives. Part 1 will examine the most recent welfare reform debates in the legislatures, highlighting the myths about women and welfare that have led Congress and the states to dismantle welfare programs without any concern for the consequences. Part 2 will describe the history of attacks on welfare, a history that makes it clear that the current drive is only the latest in a long line of assaults on poor women and the programs that serve them. Part 3 will move into the academy, where over the past fifteen years feminist scholars have struggled to "reform" the standard literature on the welfare state by bringing the lives of real women into view. And finally, Part 4 will take us from the academy into the streets where, contrary to popular wisdom, poor and middle-class women have been fighting for better social programs since the turn of the century.

But before we begin this journey, we need to understand what welfare programs in the United States were designed to do and what they have become. This part therefore begins the story by defining the many meanings of the word "welfare." It then examines the current debate to show the consequences of reform for poor and middle-class women, and explores why this discussion is happening at this particular point in time. Although I will focus on federal welfare reform, the discussion will shed light on state-level battles, which are sure to intensify as responsibility for welfare is turned back to them.

Everyone seems to agree that the welfare system is broken and needs to be fixed. However, not everyone agrees as to what ails it or how to correct its problems. Conservative critics argue that welfare is a handout that makes women dependent on government aid, and should therefore be cut back or eliminated. Liberal critics argue that welfare is necessary if poor women and children are to be cared for, and that the proposed reforms will bring them great harm. As we proceed, it will become clear that I believe that the discussion about welfare reform is not—and has never been—about welfare alone. Rather, as we shall see in what follows, politicians and policymakers regularly rediscover welfare when they cannot explain or reverse troublesome social, economic, and political trends. Poor women and welfare come under attack either because the provision of cash assistance interferes with the dynamics of the free enterprise system or because it undermines the traditional family structure. During such periods of "panic," welfare and the women receiving it are bashed in order to divert attention from the true causes of the nation's ills. It is these concerns, rather than making life better for poor women and children, that have been the driving force behind welfare reform for the past 150 years.

WHAT IS WELFARE?

During the 1930s, the collapse of the U.S. economy led to massive unemployment, major business failures, and social unrest. The turmoil shook the moorings of the capitalist system and forced Congress to provide emergency relief to all sectors of the economy. The Federal Emergency Relief Administration (FERA) and the Works Progress Administration (WPA) put cash into the empty pockets of the working poor, while other programs gave small businesses, banks, and farms a boost. This government assistance protected thousands of families from the most devastating effects of the Depression, helped to restore the public's faith in the economic and political system, and defused social unrest.

The Depression was supposed to end quickly, the relief programs were supposed to be temporary, and private charities were expected to meet the remaining demand for aid. Instead, the length and severity of the economic crisis forced Congress to acknowledge what it had preferred for so long to ignore: that market economies rarely provide enough jobs or income for everyone and that to prevent chaos and disaffection, the federal government must assume a permanent responsibility for social welfare. After considerable partisan debate, in 1935 Congress reluctantly passed the Social Security Act. This landmark legislation transferred responsibility for social welfare from the states to the federal government, replacing nineteenth-century laissez-faire economics with twentieth-century government intervention. Some thirty to fifty years after most other Western industrial nations had done so, the United States launched a modern welfare state.

The Social Security Act established two types of cash benefits: social insurance and public assistance. The social insurance programs included a pension for retired workers (what we informally call Social Security) and Unemployment Insurance, which replaces the wages of those who face temporary unemployment. Social Security is funded by a payroll tax that is paid half by the worker and half by the employer, while Unemployment Insurance is financed through a tax on the employer alone. These programs, which now cover more than 95 percent of all wage earners, have become so well accepted that most people think of them as rights, not as assistance. However, the two programs do not treat everyone equally. Both contain a "work test," for instance, that excludes low-wage and part-time workers, as well as those with limited time in the labor force, and that pays higher benefits to better paid workers with long work histories. Moreover, the Social Security payroll tax takes proportionately more from lower paid than higher paid workers.

The Social Security Act also included three public assistance programs: Aid to Dependent Children (ADC), Old Age Assistance (OAA), and Aid to the Blind (AB); Aid to the Permanently and Totally Disabled (APTD) was added in 1956. Welfare is the popular name for ADC, which provides financial assistance to children who are continuously deprived of support due to the death, absence, or incapacity of a parent or caretaker. (ADC became known as AFDC in 1962, when Congress passed a limited program for unemployed fathers and added the word "family" to reflect this change.) In 1965, Medicaid and Medicare were added to the Social Security program and in 1974 OAA, AB, and APTD were combined into a federalized income-support program called Supplemental Security Income (SSI). It was hoped that this consolidation would standardize these programs and reduce their stigma. The public assistance programs exist in all fifty states and are administered jointly by the federal government, the states, and (in some cases) the counties or cities; they are all funded largely from state and federal income taxes. Instead of the work test used by the social insurance system, the public assistance programs use an income or means test that requires applicants to prove that they are poor enough to qualify for aid. In contrast to the notion of right attached to social insurance, the public thinks of the assistance that comes from these programs as the dole.

Over time, the term welfare has gathered several interpretations. Although it was originally intended to convey the notion of well-being, today it is used to refer to many social programs and therefore lacks precision.[3] Most specifically, "welfare" refers to AFDC, and that is how it will be used in this book. But social commentators also use the word to refer (1) to *all* the public assistance programs listed above, (2) to *both* public assistance for the poor and social insurance for the middle class, and (3) even more loosely, to public assistance, social insurance, and social programs in general—that is, to the entire welfare state. The use of the word to refer to AFDC on the one hand *and* to all social programs on the other leads to a confusion that has been manipulated politically by those who would shelve these plans. For example, when critics talk about the size and cost of AFDC, they often combine its figures with those of other "welfare" programs to create the impression that AFDC is huge and expensive, and therefore deserves to be cut. Having rallied public support for axing a vaguely defined welfare program, it is then much easier to retrench Medicare, Medicaid, Food Stamps, and all the others.

The Social Security Act is one of a group of programs called "entitlements," which also include veterans' benefits, farm price supports, the Earned Income Tax Credit, federal civilian and military pensions, and the interest paid on the federal debt, as well as Food Stamps, Medicaid, and Medicare. In contrast to discretionary programs, entitlements are not subject to the vagaries of the annual budget process. Instead, Congress is required by law to fund the entitlements regardless of their cost. This fiscal guarantee created federal responsibility for social welfare and therefore laid the foundation for the modern welfare state.

During the 1980s, however, the term "entitlement" became a buzzword for something undesirable, as the Reagan administration blamed social programs for the budget deficits that had been created by its massive military spending and its tax cuts. In 1995, the Republican-led Congress mounted a frontal attack on federal entitlement programs by voting to replace many of them with state-administered block grants. This fundamental realignment of the social welfare system has once again transformed the meaning of "welfare" and unleashed unpredictable forces in the ongoing war on the poor.

SHRINKING THE WELFARE STATE

The welfare state expanded rapidly during the 1940s and 1950s, as Congress improved the Social Security Act programs and introduced new public housing, mental health, and other services. In the 1960s, the War on Poverty added Medicare, Medicaid, Food Stamps, and a host of legal, employment, social service, and anti-discrimination laws to the core income-maintenance programs. However, the expansion began to slow in the mid-1970s, once international competition, cheap foreign labor, and the loss of U.S. dominance in the world economy cut into the profits of U.S. corporations. Business executives, who had once counted on social programs to create purchasing power, maintain a healthy and educated workforce, and co-opt social movements, now declared that these same programs no longer met their goals—especially since the export of jobs and production abroad had diminished their stake in the well-being of U.S. workers. The economic security provided by social welfare programs had also strengthened the bargaining power of workers in the workplace, increased the leverage of women vis-à-vis men, and bolstered the overall political influence of social movements. None of this appealed to business leaders, who began to call for less government spending, arguing that it had raised the cost of borrowing money, increased the price of labor, deepened the deficit, and otherwise interfered with profits.[4]

Shrinking social welfare became a key feature of government plans to get the economy back on track. The campaign, begun quietly by President Carter, went into full swing when President Reagan began to openly castigate the philosophical underpinnings of the welfare state, slash social programs, and create a huge deficit that would be used to justify cuts in social welfare for years to come. President Bush continued this assault, using the slogan "No new taxes" to rationalize not raising the revenues needed to fund social programs. This was followed by Clinton's promise to "end welfare as we know it" and the Republicans' "contract" on the entire welfare state. This mounting assault on social programs—variously called supply-side economics, Reaganomics, or deficit reduction—

was therefore neither accidental nor harmless. Rather, it was part of a long-term plan to promote economic recovery by redistributing income upward, cheapening the cost of labor, shrinking social programs, and weakening the political influence of popular movements that might object to these changes.

To win support for a plan that was based on tax cuts for the rich and spending cuts for the poor and middle class, the budget cutters had to create enthusiasm for their plan among those who traditionally supported welfare and among the legions of people who stood to lose from a low minimum wage and massive cuts in health, housing, education, and social insurance. Indeed, by this time nearly 50 percent of all households depended on government benefits—from Food Stamps to Social Security to mortgage-interest tax deductions,[5] and large numbers had joined the middle class because they had found work in public sector jobs.

To create sympathy for reducing social welfare benefits, political leaders also had to destroy the belief, created after World War II, that the government should play a large role in society: they had to convince the voters that they preferred a weaker national government and a smaller welfare state. To achieve these ends, they equated tax-and-spend policies with big government and portrayed popular movements as greedy "special interests" that wanted "too much democracy." Civil rights victories were called reverse discrimination, women's rights advocates were called "bean-counters" and "femi-nazis," and single mothers, lesbians, and gay men were accused of threatening "family values."

The budget cutters turned AFDC in a major target and stalking horse for the wider attack on government spending. They backed up their assault with social science theories that blamed the poor. For example, the American Enterprise Institute, a conservative think tank with considerable influence in Washington, D.C., blamed social problems on a "culture of poverty" that promoted "defective" values and "deviant" behavior among the poor. The Institute argued that "significant numbers of American adults are not demonstrating the behavior expected of free and responsible citizens.... A substantial minority of the poor is suffering

from something more than the low income familiar in family memory to most Americans. This new thing, which we have called behavioral dependency, is more like an inability to cope." Similarly, a 1994 report published by the Heritage Foundation, another conservative think tank in Washington, claimed that while the United States may have conquered material poverty, "behavioral" poverty was "abundant and growing at an alarming pace." The report went on to define behavioral poverty as "a cluster of severe social pathologies including: an eroded work ethic and dependency, the lack of educational aspirations and achievement, an inability or unwillingness to control one's children, as well as increased single parenthood, illegitimacy, criminal activity, and drug and alcohol use."[6]

Other conservatives laid the blame for society's problems at the foot of social programs that created a "culture of entitlements." In 1987, Reagan's White House Working Group on the Family had argued that "the easy availability of welfare in all of its forms has become a powerful force for the destruction of family life through the perpetuation of a welfare culture" that discourages work and marriage, creates an unhealthy sense of entitlement, promotes dependence, and encourages people to challenge authority. More recently, the Cato Institute, another Washington research center, held that "children growing up in the welfare-ravaged neighborhoods ... are the true victims of our social welfare policies." Many, like Charles Murray, a member of the American Enterprise Institute and co-author of *The Bell Curve*, a controversial book that argues for the role of genetics in determining intelligence, took special aim at programs for single mothers: he recommended "that the AFDC payment go to zero," and that single mothers should not be eligible for subsidized housing, food stamps, or any other benefits.[7]

The liberal and radical political theories that explain the development of the welfare state from the 1930s through the mid-1970s take a very different view. Liberals believe that the roots of social problems lie in flawed institutions, not in the flawed values and behavior of individuals or in overtly permissive social programs. Liberal policies thus target the lack of equal opportunity rather than poor attitudes or the absence of personal values. On the grounds that living and working in an industrial society leaves people vulnerable to the loss of income due to old age, joblessness, illness, or family dissolution, liberals see social welfare programs as a necessary and appropriate protection against conditions over which individuals have little or no control. In fact, many Western industrial nations go further and define such protections as the universal *right* of all members of a society—although in these countries too, welfare programs are increasingly coming under attack.

Radicals, on the other hand, argue that poverty is an inevitable feature of profit-driven economies based on private ownership of the means of production and the exploitation of labor. Thus the social structure, not individual behavior or malfunctioning institutions, leads to an unequal distribution of money and power. However, when proposing remedies, radicals do not always agree that social programs are the best solution. Some believe that welfare programs cool out protest movements and therefore co-opt the working class.[8] Others believe that the economic back-up provided by social programs can, if substantial enough, increase the political leverage of marginalized groups and position them to take the risks needed to resist exploitation on the job and subordination in the home. In other words, the welfare state is a potential arena for progressive political struggle between the haves and have-nots, as well as a site of social control.[9]

THE WAR ON WELFARE

The debate over welfare has included four major assaults on poor women and AFDC. The first round was directed at the program's growth and cost; the second targeted women's work behavior; the third focussed on women's childbearing choices; and the fourth (and most recent) has taken aim at these programs' entitlement status and at the role of the federal government in administering them. As we will see below, all of these assaults are fueled by negative stereotypes of both poor women and welfare, and none can pass the test of empirical research or even common sense. Instead, they serve the political agendas of politicians seeking to win votes.

The first assault took the form of cutbacks. Following the "explosion" of the welfare rolls in the late 1960s (described in detail in Part 2), the number of people on welfare stabilized: the AFDC program served between 3 and 4 million families (or 10 to 11 million individuals) throughout the 1970s and 1980s, even though more people were poor.[10] Ignoring the data, President Reagan introduced the 1981 Omnibus Budget Reconciliation Act (OBRA), which cut AFDC by lowering benefits and tightening eligibility rules—since AFDC is an entitlement program, its funding could not simply be reduced. These changes nevertheless pushed thousands of women into low-paid jobs, dangerous welfare hotels, drug-plagued streets, and unsafe relationships; they also shrunk the public sector workforce, undoubtedly forcing some of the women who lost jobs to apply for AFDC.

The budget cutters billed AFDC as a program that had grown out of control and argued that welfare was responsible for the nation's economic problems. They played to the middle class's perception of welfare as something draining the Treasury, wasting funds on bloated bureaucracies, allowing women to live high on the hog, and fueling the deficit. Yet the facts suggest otherwise. For one, except during economic downturns, the growth of AFDC had basically kept pace with population growth: it has *always* served between 11 and 13 percent of all children, and less than 5 percent of the total population. And although AFDC spending had indeed grown, it could hardly be held responsible for draining the Treasury or fueling the deficit: in 1983, the $22 billion spent on AFDC, Supplemental Security Income, and Food Stamps combined accounted for only 3.8 percent of the federal budget. In contrast, 19.8 percent went to Social Security, 22.8 percent to discretionary defense spending, and 8.9 percent to net interest payments on the federal debt. As for bureaucratic waste, in 1981, $12 billion of the $14 billion AFDC budget was spent on benefits to recipients, and only $1.6 billion—or 7 percent—on administration, down from 17 percent in 1970. Further, the median AFDC benefit (adjusting for inflation) *declined* 37 percent between 1970 and 1980. The average benefit in 1980 was $274 a month for a family of three, or a pitiful 50 percent of the $6,565 official poverty-line income for a family of that size.[11]

Then, as today, welfare critics tried to fortify their claim that AFDC consumes vast amounts of money by arguing that these numbers understate the recipients' income because many of them also receive Food Stamps and Medicaid. But while those receiving Food Stamps do have more disposable income each month, the dollar amount is small; and it is deceptive to count the much larger cost of Medicaid as personal income since these payments go directly to doctors and hospitals. The IRS certainly does not count the healthcare bills paid by insurance companies as the personal income of the middle class. Moreover, including Medicaid as personal income when evaluating poverty status creates the paradox that a poor person's income would rise when Medicaid reimbursed a hospital for a long and costly stay and fall when that person regained his or her health.

While the 1981 act did reduce the number of welfare recipients, it only did so temporarily. An average of 659,000 more people received AFDC in 1990 and each of the next four years, the result of falling wages (average weekly earnings, adjusted for inflation, fell almost 19 percent from 1972 to 1995)[12] and disappearing jobs (due to de-industrialization, corporate downsizing, and the exportation of production abroad). By 1993, nearly 5 million families (14.2 million individuals) were receiving AFDC. Although government spending on the program had risen to $25.7 billion by that time, it still accounted for only 1 percent of the federal budget—3.4 percent when Food Stamps and Supplemental Security Income are included. And by November 1994 the number of recipients had fallen to 13.9 million, due to economic recovery on the one hand and tightened eligibility rules on the other. In July 1995, the national AFDC caseload was 6.4 percent lower than the 1994 average.[13]

Yet this decrease had no effect on the debate over welfare reform. Nor did the reformers mention that the $25 billion spent on AFDC in 1994 was small compared to the approximately $104.3 billion spent on the 125 federal subsidies and tax breaks for U.S. corporations.[14] Instead, they used welfare as a code word for big government and called for further cuts, along with additional budget-busting tax breaks for the rich. Meanwhile, in 1993 nearly half the national income—48.2 percent—went to the top fifth of households (the highest proportion recorded to date), while the share of income going to the bottom fifth dropped to its lowest level ever—3.6 percent.[15]

ENFORCING THE WORK ETHIC

The second assault on welfare focussed on women's work behavior. From 1935 until the late 1960s, it was expected that women, especially mothers of young children, would stay at home. Federal AFDC policy enforced this gender norm by requiring the states to penalize AFDC mothers who became employed. Some states, however, wanted to keep poor women available for the local low-wage labor market, and got around the rules by lowering their benefits and restricting eligibility. When, in the early 1970s, the rapid expansion of the service sector further increased the demand for women workers, the federal government also tried to force women off welfare. By the early 1980s, business and government were convinced that access to welfare was leading poor women to avoid work. At the same time, the ideas of the women's movement, changing views of women's roles, and the entry of large numbers of middle-class women into the workforce made it easier for the government to require that poor women on welfare go to work. These changing attitudes fueled support for the welfare cuts made under OBRA in 1981, as well as the incentives it gave to the states to experiment with welfare-to-work programs.

By the mid-1980s, the continued growth of low-paid service sector jobs was leading business experts to predict that by the year 2000, labor markets would be "tighter than at any time in recent history."[16] In 1986, the National Alliance of Business (NAB) concluded that "welfare recipients represent an important source of needed workers" that must be encouraged to enter the labor market through government-subsidized education, training, and social services. The NAB added, "No sector [of the economy] can afford a growing underclass that cannot get or keep jobs, nor can the nation afford to suffer losses in productivity and world competitiveness because workers are unprepared for changes in the workplace."[17] These corporate concerns reflected both a need for employees in general and a fear that labor shortages would make it more difficult to recruit women in particular: up to this point, few companies did much to accommodate women's concerns about unequal pay, health benefits, and family responsibilities.

The 1988 Family Support Act officially transformed welfare from a program designed in 1935 to help single mothers stay home with their children into a program that mandated work as a condition of receiving aid. Both liberals and conservatives heralded it as the most important welfare reform in two decades. Its centerpiece, the Job Opportunity and Basic Security (JOBS) program, required that recipients be working, searching for a job, or preparing for employment. A woman who refused to go to work or enter an education or training program risked having her benefits reduced or terminated. To ease the transition to employment, the JOBS program provided AFDC mothers with a year of childcare services and Medicaid coverage. To maintain their federal matching funds, the states had to have 15 percent of their AFDC caseload enrolled in the JOBS program by 1995.

The work and family supports created by JOBS helped women while eliminating the pressure on business to provide such benefits. However, their coercive character reflected the policymakers' deep-seated distrust of poor women's willingness to work. For example, after acknowledging that the economy fails some people for a time, the 1987 American Enterprise Institute report cited earlier concluded that "the most disturbing element among a fraction of the contemporary poor is an inability to seize opportunity even when it is available.... Some may have work skills in the normal sense, but find it difficult to be regular, prompt and in a sustained way attentive to their work. Their need is less for job training than for meaning and order in their lives."[18] Yet if the reformers had believed that women were interested in working, they could have found other ways to make employment economically more attractive than AFDC—for instance, by allowing recipients to keep a greater portion of their benefits when they also worked, or by pressing Congress to raise the minimum wage. But such non-coercive options did not see the light of day because helping women to combine welfare and wages into one package risked increasing the welfare rolls, while granting a higher minimum wage or insisting on health benefits risked antagonizing employers.

Bill Clinton's 1992 campaign pledge "to end welfare as we know it" forced him to call for even stricter work requirements than those imposed through the Family Support Act. Clinton therefore proposed that the JOBS program be turned into a *transitional* and *temporary* program by requiring all able-bodied recipients to go to work after two years on welfare. To keep his campaign promise and establish his conservative credentials, Clinton also encouraged the states to experiment with time-limited work programs and other "reforms," offering to waive any federal rules they violated. Between February 1993 and September 1994—long before the current round of welfare legislation—Clinton's Department of Health and Human Services granted nineteen states requests for waivers of the time limit rule—nearly all that applied.

Clinton's Work and Responsibility Act, unveiled in June 1994, made time-limited welfare benefits federal policy—even though official unemployment was about 18 percent in inner-city neighborhoods, where about 40 percent of the population lived below the poverty line.[19] Clinton spoke of job guarantees and promised to double federal spending for the education, job training, and childcare assistance that would be available before the two-year time limit expired. But he also wanted to put those unable to find work within the two years in a "workfare" program—euphemistically called a community service job—where they would be required to work off their AFDC benefits by cleaning parks and office buildings. In the majority of instances, the resulting wage-equivalent would fall far below the minimum wage.[20]

The November 1994 Congressional elections, which swept Newt Gingrich (R-GA) and his fellow Republicans into power, changed the terms of the debate. While Clinton's welfare reform bill had not yet become law, his rhetoric had opened the door to even more draconian proposals. The final bill had not been passed at the time this book went to press, but most observers expect that it will include a limit on the time that a woman can receive welfare (probably five years) regardless of family circumstances; participation in some kind of work or community service for a specified number of hours a week (up to thirty-five) after two years on welfare (earlier at state option); and few if any supports—childcare, education, training, and the reimbursement of work-related expenses—that make it possible for women to go to work. In addition, by the year 2000, any state that wants to retain full federal funding will have to move half its welfare recipients into a job or job-search activity, even though most states have failed to meet the current 15 percent participation rate.[21] The Clinton administration has estimated that, depending on its severity, such a bill could push between 1 and 2 million children into poverty.

Myths About Women, Welfare, and Work

The United States is proud of its work ethic—Americans believe that people who can find work ought to—and as a result, welfare and work have always been linked. We can see how the link is a particularly capitalist one, however, when we realize that calls for welfare reform crop up at times when women are using the welfare system as an alternative to dirty, dangerous, and low-paying jobs. Thus it is at those moments when wages fall below the welfare grant or when employers want to increase the supply of low-paid workers that policymakers try to reform welfare to make sure that only the most desperate choose it over employment.

Thus in the current debate, welfare critics have focussed on women's work behavior and justified their assault by invoking negative, unfounded, and often racialized stereotypes of poor women. For instance, they have claimed that welfare recipients do not want to work for wages, that they are lazy and need the strong arm of the government to make them change their ways. As one example, Governor Kirk Fordice of Mississippi was reported to have declared that "the only job training that welfare recipients need is a good alarm clock." Lawrence Mead, a conservative political scientist, concluded that "the poor remain economically passive in a society where other low-skilled people find abundant opportunity." Robert Rector, a policy analyst with the Heritage Foundation, told Congress that if everyone would simply "finish high school, get a job, any job, and stick with it and not have children outside of marriage, no one would be poor." [22]

Despite evidence that the labor market can neither absorb all those willing and able to work nor pay a living wage to everyone who needs one, these welfare opponents insist that work empowers poor women, raises their self-esteem, and provides them with a sense of control over their lives. However, if they had been asked, the women on welfare would have told the reformers that the reality is far more complex. Until the mid-1970s, a full-time, full-year job paying the federal minimum wage could lift a worker out of poverty, but that has not been the case in any year since. As one thirty-seven-year-old New Jersey JOBS participant put it, "How are you supposed to survive on the minimum wage—feed the kids, pay the rent, utilities?"[23]

Take the example of April. She comes from a middle-class family. After her boyfriend left her to raise their two children alone, she took a job working the swing shift in a nursing home. After three months she was forced to leave because the job "wasn't even paying my bills. At the end of the week I'd get a check for less than $100. Daycare cost $75. I'd have $10 to eat and $10 to put gas in the car so I could get back and forth to this useless job." Another woman agreed: "It's like a roller coaster. Once you get up there, you realize you can't pay for medical, you can't pay for childcare, you can't pay for your transportation and then you wonder why you are working. It doesn't make sense why you're putting in all these hours of work and you're not getting anywhere. It's like a vicious cycle that everyone gets caught up in."[24]

Years of academic research confirm what these women are saying—that women on welfare desperately want to work or are *already* working—and puts the situation in a larger perspective. Using longitudinal data, LaDonna Pavetti, a researcher at the John F. Kennedy School of Government, found that 70 percent of women who receive AFDC leave the rolls within two years, either to work

or to marry, and that only 7 percent stay for more than eight years. She also reported that while unstable jobs, lack of childcare and health benefits, and failed relationships sent a significant number of women back onto AFDC within five years, most of the returnees only used welfare as a short-term economic back-up during a crisis. A small number did need assistance for longer than eight years, but these tended to be single mothers of young children who were school drop-outs with little work experience, or women who were too ill or disabled to work at all.[25]

A study by the Washington, D.C.-based Institute for Women's Policy Research (IWPR) found that the average AFDC mother works about 950 hours a year, approximately the same as all mothers in the workforce; that over 40 percent of women on welfare "package" AFDC with wages, either simultaneously or sequentially; and that an additional 30 percent spend substantial time looking for work but cannot find it. The IWPR also reported that the state of the local labor market made a big difference: welfare mothers living in states with unemployment rates of 10 percent or more had only a 13 percent chance of finding jobs, while those in states where unemployment was 3.5 percent or less had a 29 percent chance. In addition, many working welfare mothers hold sporadic full-time jobs rather than steady part-time ones, and the majority are in low-wage "women's occupations."[26]

Even those women who found jobs did not earn enough to make ends meet. Although three-quarters of the single mothers who received AFDC during the two-year period studied by the IWPR were in the paid labor force, few worked enough hours or earned enough to lift their families out of poverty. These women earned an average of $4.29 an hour (in 1990 dollars) on their primary job, compared to $10.03 for non-farm private sector employees in 1990. The IWPR researchers concluded that "recipients use AFDC for many reasons, including to supplement their low-wage work effort and to provide a safety net during periods of unemployment, disability, and family crises." While AFDC may need to be reformed because of its inadequacies, it "cannot be eliminated without causing great harm to already impoverished families."[27] These findings have been confirmed by other well-known studies of welfare-to-work programs, which conclude that most recipients would readily leave welfare if they could—in other words, if there were enough jobs with decent wages and such benefits as childcare and healthcare.[28]

The welfare critics also downplay the difficulties women have balancing work and family. Indeed, only half of all mothers with young children—even those with husbands—work at all, and many only work part time. Work does indeed provide important personal and social benefits, but working in a dirty, dangerous, demeaning, and low-paid job does not guarantee a positive outcome. Yet reforms that will require that a certain percent of a state's caseload be off welfare and at work will throw millions of women into the labor force. According to the Economic Policy Institute, swelling the labor pool in this way could lead to a more than 10 percent decline in the wages of low-paid workers—more in states with larger welfare populations, such as New York (an estimated 17.1 percent decline) and California (an estimated 17.8

percent decline). In five states, wages could end up below the federal minimum.[29] Unions, especially those representing public employees, have been especially concerned about this, but effective guarantees against their members being displaced in this way do not appear in the reform bills.

Some reformers do recognize that welfare alone is not enough, but it is doubtful that the few supplements they favor will help welfare mothers unless they are modified to take women's work and family life into account. For instance, neither the Earned Income Tax Credit (EITC—a tax rebate for the working poor) nor Unemployment Insurance supports people who are not in the labor force or who stay home to raise children. A woman who packaged EITC and part-time or temporary work would be *less* well off financially than if she combined AFDC and the same job.[30] Furthermore, Congress, in its rush to weaken all federal programs, has put even the highly touted EITC on the chopping block. In today's economy, Clinton's promise "to make work pay for those who try hard and play by the rules" rings hollow for women on welfare. One New York AFDC recipient explained, "You need real jobs for people ... throwing people off welfare won't work, how are they going to get jobs if they are in the streets?" Testifying at a Connecticut hearing, a thirty-two-year-old woman who has had to alternate between menial jobs and welfare said, "I have no problem working, but the skills I have are not enough." A welfare mother in Oregon focused on the larger picture: "Women are supposed to fill all the minimum-wage jobs in this country," she declared. Like other women on welfare, she realized that pushing mothers off AFDC into low-paid jobs benefits businesses and politicians, but keeps women in "their place."[31]

UPHOLDING THE FAMILY ETHIC

The third assault has been on women's marital, childbearing, and parenting behavior. Indeed, welfare reform has been governed by a "family ethic" as well as a work ethic. According to the American "family ethic," or set of beliefs about how families should operate, people should marry and live in two-parent households, preferably with one wage earner and one homemaker. All other family types are considered deviant. Realizing that this is a patriarchal concept of the family will help us understand why calls for welfare reform often arise alongside public concerns about changes in women's roles and in the structure of the family. For instance, in recent years conservative social scientists have associated rising rates of nonmarital births with the "breakdown" of the family and have deplored the "reproductive deviance" of poor women.[32] Stuart Butler and Anna Kondratas charge that AFDC finances "a subculture of people" who want children but not marriage, who disdain family commitments, and "who downplay the importance of male figures." The typical AFDC parent today, they say, is not the worthy widow envisaged in the original legislation but the divorced, deserted, or never-married woman. Charles Murray has declared that "illegitimacy is the single most important social problem of our time—more important than crime, drugs, poverty, illiteracy, welfare, or homelessness, because it drives everything else." He concludes that single mothers drain community resources, destroy the community's capacity to sustain itself, and should therefore not be given economic support.

Beneath all this rhetoric lies the patriarchal premise that any family without a father is defective. As one expert who testified a few years ago about the impact of welfare on families concluded, "Raised in an environment in which fathers don't provide for the young and dependency on government is assumed, few children will develop the skills of self-sufficiency, or even the concept of personal responsibility. Young men will not strive to be good providers, and young women will not expect it of their men."[33]

Many politicians from both political parties agree that all kinds of social problems—from poverty to crime to the deficit—stem from this decline in "family values." To underscore this point, they have resurrected such long-discredited terms as "unfit" mothers and "illegitimate" children, and have associated single parenthood with a decline in morality. For instance, both the Democratic and Republican welfare plans link eligibility for AFDC to compliance with certain standards of marital, childbearing, and parenting behavior, penalizing women who depart from certain prescribed wife and mother roles.

Single mothers are punished in at least three ways. First, there is the highly controversial child exclusion, also called the family cap because it denies AFDC to children who are born while their mothers are receiving AFDC and to unmarried teen mothers and their children. If a woman insists on becoming pregnant, the lawmakers tell her that she should turn to relatives, apply for charity, or place her child in an orphanage—ignoring the fact that these cost an average of $36,500 per child per year. Second, paternity penalties are stiffened. States are required to withhold some benefits from mothers who refuse to help identify the child's father, as well as from mothers who cooperate with the authorities but fail to establish paternity due to bureaucratic red tape or the father's ability to conceal his whereabouts. While establishing paternity can help children to gain access to child support and Social Security survivor's benefits, these unduly restrictive procedures penalize women for not having men in the home and at the same time place their children in harm's way. In fact, one estimate suggests that enforcement of the paternity rule would throw nearly 30 percent of children off the AFDC rolls.[34] Third, there is an "illegitimacy" bonus—extra federal money for states that lower their nonmarital birth *and* abortion rates.[35]

These efforts to regulate marriage, childbearing, and parenting began in the states. As he did with time limits, President Clinton encouraged the states to develop their own child exclusion and "parenting" programs by waiving federal rules that prevented such actions. As of November 1995, the Department of Health and Human Services had authorized thirteen child exclusion waivers, with several more in the pipeline.[36] In addition, Florida and Ohio have already proposed a cash bonus for mothers who agree to use Norplant (the long-lasting but controversial contraceptive implant), along with a separate plan to reward fathers who have vasectomies, while Colorado has considered penalizing women on welfare who refuse family planning counseling and Utah has reviewed a plan to pay $3,000 to unwed pregnant women who carry their babies to term and put them up for adoption.[37] Both state and federal reform proposals also include such programs as Learnfare, which docks the checks of AFDC mothers whose children are truant, and Healthfare, which lowers the AFDC grant if children are not immunized on a prescribed schedule.

When such measures are imposed as a *condition* of aid, they take advantage of a woman's dire financial situation, leaving her with little choice but to trade her health, as well as her contraceptive, religious, and parenting preferences, for an AFDC check. This type of economic coercion presumes that poor women are unable to make their own reproductive decisions and therefore must be subjected to the strong arm of the government. Knowing about these state-level initiatives is important: should AFDC become a block grant program, we can expect that more states will enact such measures to control "reproductive deviance."

Myths About Women, Welfare, and Childbearing

Like the welfare reforms that target women's work behavior, these efforts to control their reproductive behavior have been fueled by numerous myths and stereotypes, all of which have repeatedly been proved wrong by researchers. It has been suggested, for example, that AFDC is responsible for changes in family structure—not only the declining rate of marriage and the rise of single-mother households, but also the increase in the nonmarital birth rate. In fact, neither poor women nor welfare can be held responsible for changes in family patterns that have spread throughout society and affected women in all walks of life.

Marriage: One myth is that AFDC breaks up families. Even though AFDC rules disqualify most two-parent families, the program does not *create* single-parent households. Welfare critics say AFDC causes marriages to break up because the program for single parents sometimes leads men to move out so their families can survive. But research, psychological knowledge, and plain commonsense suggest that even poor people marry and divorce for a host of reasons that have nothing whatsoever to do with the availability of an AFDC check. Indeed, in 1993 half of *all* women in the United States between the ages of fifteen and forty-four were not married; compared to earlier periods, people are getting married later, divorcing and separating more, and are less likely to remarry and more likely to cohabit. Moreover, the number of one-parent families with children more than doubled between 1970 and 1993, while those with two parents *fell*, from 87.1 percent to 73 percent. As a result, single parents headed 27 percent of all families with children in 1993, up from only 12.8 percent in 1970. More than half of all children born today will be raised by only one parent during a part of their lifetimes. And while single motherhood is more prevalent in the black community than in the white, those who hold welfare responsible rarely note that two-thirds of all single parents are white.[38]

Fears about women and marriage have been projected onto AFDC as fewer and fewer mother-only families, both on AFDC and throughout society, are headed by widows—still the most socially acceptable basis for a mother-only family—while more and more are headed by *never-married* women.[39] As for the racial breakdown, from 1976 to 1992 blacks comprised the majority of never-married recipients, although the proportion declined (from 71 to 51 percent), while the proportion of white families in this category rose (from 19 to 27 percent). As a result, the racial composition of never-married women on welfare increasingly resembles that of all never-married women.[40]

Childbearing: Another myth about the effect of AFDC on family life is that poor women have kids for money. In fact, women on AFDC have lower fertility rates than women in the general population. Further, the average family on welfare includes a mother and two children, which is also the average for the nation. Forty-three percent of today's AFDC households have only one child and 30 percent have two.[41] Since a women must have at least one child to qualify for AFDC in the first place, and since most women have only one more child while on the rolls, welfare can hardly be considered to *cause* large families. In any case, many women at all income levels have unintended pregnancies, suggesting the futility of bonuses and penalties.[42] Moreover, the states only provide an average of about $60 a month for each additional child, barely enough to pay for milk and diapers. A more efficient and humane way to lower the nonmarital birth rate than shrinking the already skimpy AFDC grant would be to focus on pregnancy prevention, sex education in the schools, and providing access to family planning and abortion services.

In 1994, seventy-nine social scientists issued a press release to refute the notion that the availability of welfare determined a women's childbearing decisions.[43] These scholars pointed out, for instance, that states with more stringent welfare rules do *not* have fewer nonmarital pregnancies. On the contrary, some states with low benefits have very high nonmarital birth rates. Those few studies that have reported an association between higher benefits and nonmarital births found only a slight connection, and that was only for whites. Moreover, the nonmarital birth rate for all women rose from 26 per 1,000 live births in 1970 to 44 per 1,000 in 1990, while the value of the AFDC grant plummeted by 36 percent in the same period.[44] And while child exclusion advocates argue that workers' wages do not automatically rise when they have children, in fact workers receive an additional tax exemption for each new dependent, and many can still count on an annual pay raise when they plan to expand their families. Child exclusion supporters who fear that AFDC payments invite women to have children do not worry that the income tax exemption for dependents, the Earned Income Tax Credit for families with children, and the proposed $500 tax credit per child will lead other working- and middle-class families to have kids "for money."

As for the controversial teen mother group, in 1992, 5 percent of single women receiving AFDC were teen mothers, up from 2 percent in 1976. Women who gave birth as teenagers made up 42 percent of the AFDC caseload—but this proportion has

remained roughly the same throughout the seventeen-year period, even though the nonmarital birth rate among *all* teenagers has increased steadily.[45] Not only are nonmarital births more common for women in their twenties, but teenage girls often become pregnant by men age twenty or older.[46]

Parenting: A third myth about AFDC's impact on family life is that it undermines effective parenting. The view of single-parent families as "broken" or "deviant" reflects the long-standing distrust of women who raise children without men as heads of the household, especially if the women are poor, non-white, or foreign born. Part 2 reviews how this thinking rationalized breaking up families and institutionalizing children in years past. The same negative thinking fuels today's proposals to place children in foster care or orphanages if their mothers cannot find work. In 1994, Myron Magnet of the conservative Manhattan Institute declared, "Anyone who looks at underclass children— neglected, abused, unimmunized, deprived of the moral and cognitive nurturing that families provide—has to ask whose welfare is advanced by a system that consigns so many children to emotional and intellectual stunting and to likely failure in school and later life." From the child's point of view, he added, "an incompetent mother on crack is not better than a Dickensian orphanage." Magnet then recommended that poor children and their mothers be placed in community hostels that would provide them with "the whole array of cognitive and moral categories that one is supposed to learn at home."[47] The effects of this argument, which generalizes from individual instances of self-destructive behavior to all poor women on welfare, can be seen in the current welfare reform bills, which preserve unlimited federal support for children who have been removed from their homes to shelters, foster homes, or institutions. Based on what is happening in states (such as Wisconsin) that have already made drastic AFDC cuts, child-protection officials predict that even before the federal reforms are in place, changes at the state level will flood the child welfare system.[48]

Distrust of the ability of poor women to socialize their children (which must sound odd to the women hired to take care of children in middle- and upper class homes) clearly underlies such state and federal programs as Learnfare and Healthfare, which use threats to reduce AFDC checks as a way to teach recipients how to parent "responsibly." The value of attending school and visiting the doctor goes without saying, yet Learnfare's own evaluators concluded that "a troubling large number of teens described their schools as dangerous and frightening places where learning was difficult and recommended both educational and welfare reform."[49] Improving the public schools and increasing access to healthcare would help poor parents far more than any get-tough "personal responsibility bill." And where parental guidance is needed—as it may be in some cases—positive outreach works better than threats of punishment by the state.

The campaign to wring child support from "deadbeat dads" targets the parenting behavior of poor men. Child-support advocates argue that revoking the driving (or professional) licenses of absent fathers who do not pay up will turn them into responsible providers *and* reduce welfare costs. Critics contend that overly strenuous child-support efforts could jeopardize the relationships that many AFDC fathers are able, sometimes with difficulty, to maintain with their children. They also warn that the aggressive pursuit of child support may expose women to male violence. Child-support enforcement will in any case produce only minimal funds because poor women partner with poor men and because most of the funds collected go directly to the state.

The truth is that, in the name of increasing parental responsibility, most of the current welfare reform proposals will make it harder for poor women to parent. For one thing, reducing benefits and increasing poverty only adds to family stress. Time limits and mandatory work programs not only devalue a woman's caretaking work, but leave children unsupervised in neighborhoods that have inadequate schools, substandard housing, lack of medical services, and may be plagued by drugs, crime, and violence. A Wisconsin welfare mother avoided attending a job-search program while she was going to school so that she could have time to spend with her kids. While her caseworker believed that she could do both, she said, "I know I can, but who would my kids be eating dinner with? Who would put them to bed if I were to work nights and go to school during the day? Even AFDC kids need their moms." Speaking about her efforts to cope after her brother was killed by a stray bullet, a Massachusetts woman explained, "I would walk the girls to the bus, then I would walk to the train and go to work. I would call home about 3:00 pm; my mother was supposed to be home when the girls came home. And if they were not home, I would be frantic. It was so hard, I was going nuts."[50]

If the welfare reformers had bothered to ask the women who receive AFDC, they would have found that they turn to welfare in order to better care for their children. Many years after leaving AFDC, Lynn Woolsey (D-CA), the only former welfare mother ever to serve in Congress, told the *New York Times*, "I know what it is like to lie awake at night and worry about not having any health insurance. I know how hard it is to find good childcare. I had thirteen different baby sitters in one year. I know what it is like to choose between paying the rent and buying new shoes. Like so many American families, we turned to AFDC."[51]

The idea that a female-dominated welfare culture keeps families trapped on welfare from generation to generation is another myth about AFDC that is unsupported by the research. Longitudinal studies indicate that while women from welfare families are more likely than women from non-welfare families to receive AFDC as adults, most women who receive welfare as children do not turn to the program when they grow up.[52] Those studies that found links between welfare and "intergenerational dependency" did not control for income—leaving it unclear whether daughters of welfare mothers turn to AFDC because they received public assistance as children or because they never escaped poverty.

The evidence suggests that it is *living in poverty*, not welfare, that can lead to families to break up and can bring harm to children, and most women on AFDC were poor before they became recipients. When low wages and high unemployment prevent men from carrying out their breadwinner roles, fewer men and women want to, or can, marry. This is especially true in the African-American community, where racism takes a heavy economic toll. Economic insecurity can also lead marriages to dissolve. In any case, marriage is not every woman's preference; nor is it necessarily an effective anti-poverty strategy. While two incomes are usually better than one, the sad truth is that many women remain poor even if they tie the knot: two-earner households are one of the nation's fastest growing poverty groups.

Poverty, rather than a welfare check, can also harm children.[53] Poverty reduces the chance of getting an education and a job, limits economic mobility, and negatively affects health and self-esteem. The pressure placed on adults who have to juggle employment and childcare, find adequate housing, and manage small incomes can place children at risk of parental abuse. Those who link welfare to negative behavior often fail to take the role of poverty into account—even though everyone on welfare is poor. Since social problems do appear more frequently among poor families and since single mothers (whether never-married or divorced) do tend to be poor, blaming poverty on welfare conveniently deflects attention from its roots in the economy.

ATTACKING ENTITLEMENTS

The most recent, and potentially far-reaching, assault on AFDC is the proposal to strip it of its entitlement status through block grants that will turn its administration back to the states. Block grants first came into vogue during the Nixon administration and were expanded under Reagan. These early efforts paved the way for the Contract With America, which puts block grants at the center of its reforms. Billed as a way to free the states from "burdensome" federal rules, block grants will not only abolish nearly sixty years of federal responsibility for cash assistance to the poor, but are likely to be the first step in the dismantling of the entire welfare state—and thus in the end affect the middle class as well as the poor.

As noted earlier, the entitlement programs offer more protection than programs funded by block grants because their appropriations are automatically renewed each year. In exchange for federal support, the states must follow federal guidelines, including the mandate to serve all qualified applicants. The block grant approach will destroy this safety net by undermining the funding guarantee: block grants will be subject to the annual budget process, which removes the promise of fixed funding levels and the assurance that Congress will increase funding should inflation, recession, population growth, or other conditions increase the cost of public assistance. For example, the proposed Temporary Family Assistance Block Grant (which replaces AFDC and other programs for poor families) authorizes funding for only five years and proposes to spend 15 percent less than what the Congressional Budget Office predicted the program would have cost by the year 2001 under the old law. In addition, block grants eliminate the states' obligation to fully match federal funds. At present, the states must commit their own resources in order to receive federal dollars—on average, 45 percent of the total cost of AFDC. Without this mandate, a state whose demand for cash aid exceeded its resources would face such unpalatable choices as raising taxes, using existing state funds to meet the additional demand, cutting benefits, denying aid to the newly poor, creating a waiting list, or ending cash assistance altogether.[54]

Block grants also undermine the safety net by earmarking federal funds so loosely that they can be spent on any low-income program, and not necessarily on AFDC. In addition, the state can choose to provide aid in the form of vouchers, goods, or services, rather than cash. The block grant legislation also expressly forbids spending on certain individuals, based on the length of time they have been receiving AFDC, as well as their marital, citizenship, or paternity status. The current state waivers foreshadow what is to come. Some states have used them to improve AFDC—for instance, by allowing families to keep more of their income and assets and by opening the program to more two-parent households. However, according to the New York-based Center on Social Welfare Policy and Law—a well-known a legal services organization that has been monitoring welfare policy for more than twenty years—most of the experiments pose a significant risk of harm to some or all family members involved.[55] As of November 1995, most of the waivers were used to impose time limits, mandate work, deny aid to children born on welfare, and reduce benefits to families whose children rehave not attended school regularly or who have not been properly immunized.

Finally, the block grants erode the safety net by eliminating most federal accountability and oversight. The entitlement system has provided the United States with a overarching set of standards that apply to public assistance programs in every state. At the same time, the states have retained considerable flexibility, including the right to define "need," to set their own benefit levels, and to establish certain rules. Block grants limit federal regulation and break an integrated system into fifty separate parts. Critics fear that the decentralization will encourage the states to compete with each other to offer the lowest AFDC benefit. They also worry that existing inequities—benefits range from a high of $923 in Alaska to a low of $120 in Mississippi—will be exacerbated if the current penalty for reducing benefits below the May 1988 level is removed. The (unproved) belief that higher benefits attract welfare migration from neighboring states has led client advocates to worry that block grants will lead to a "race to the bottom" among the states.

Block grants also encourage the states to shift costs on down to the counties, which will surely touch off conflicts between state and local officials. As the worried president of the National Association of Elected County Officials put it, "If a mom is forced to go to work and does not have childcare, the county will seize the child. Not only is that a human tragedy, but the county will pay the bill. And the state and federal government will be completely protected because they have capped all the risk."[56] Thus although block grants are billed as a way to make government more democratic, governors and state legislators will face intensified lobbying from competing low-income constituencies fighting for their share of a single block grant—a process known for marginalizing powerless groups.

THE WAR ON WELFARE CONCERNS ALL WOMEN

Welfare reform harms women on AFDC for being poor and raising children on their own. But the proposed reforms threaten the rights of *all* women to decent pay, to control over their own sexuality, to a life free of abusive relationships, and to a choice of families that do not fit the two-parent model. They do this by weakening women's caretaking supports, threatening their reproductive rights, and undercutting their independence.

Caretaking supports: As noted earlier, welfare reform has become a launching pad for a wider attack on all of the nation's social welfare programs. The impact of the attack has been compounded by the drive to balance the budget by the year 2002. Since slashing programs for the poor will yield less than 10 percent of the savings needed, many more government programs will have to be cut back to fill the projected $1.4 trillion budget gap.[57] Yet many health, education, childcare, social service, and social security programs, as well as tax expenditures (i.e., mortgage-interest deductions, childcare credits, etc.), help all but the most affluent families by reducing the cost of basic consumption items, helping pay health and education bills, and providing for those who cannot support themselves. Yet the attack on welfare legitimizes both cutting all social programs and shifting the cost of caretaking from the government to women at a time when they need more, not fewer, family supports.

Reproductive rights: The attack on poor women's reproductive choices undermines the reproductive rights of all women. Shortly after 1973, when the Supreme Count (in Roe *v.* Wade) granted women the right to an abortion, the right-to-life forces won passage of the Hyde Amendment, which forbids the use of Medicaid dollars for abortions. Today, poor women in two-thirds of the states lack access to this service except in cases of rape or incest, and even this exception is under attack. The current use of economic coercion to control the childbearing decisions of poor women on welfare broadens the attempt by government to control women's reproductive lives; it also implicitly endorses efforts by abortion foes to deny more women access to abortion, either by introducing piecemeal restrictions (such as the called-for ban on abortions for military wives, women prisoners, and federal employee insurance beneficiaries) or by passing a constitutional amendment.

Economic independence: The attack on welfare threatens the economic independence of all women by making it harder to earn an adequate living. For one, a smaller welfare state means fewer of the public-sector jobs that enabled many women—both white women and women-of-color—to enter the middle class. Second, low benefits ensure that only the most desperate women will choose welfare over work, while time limits and workfare channel large numbers of low-paid female workers into the labor market; both will increase the competition for jobs and depress women's wages. Third, the reform proposals virtually eliminate all support for high school and college education, two widely accepted routes off welfare and out of poverty. And finally, the reforms undercut the role of AFDC as an economic back-up, making it easier for employers to keep women in line by evoking fears of unemployment. The economic security provided by AFDC also permits women to take the risks associated with resisting male domination in the home.

WHY NOW?

We have seen how the drive to undermine welfare has relied on myths about the relationship between welfare and women's work, marital, childbearing, and parenting behavior to build support for reforms that contradict research findings, labor market realities, and the dynamics of family life. But why is welfare being attacked right now? What purpose does demonizing poor women and impugning welfare serve?

Simply put, attacking welfare and the women who receive it eases the economic, moral, and racial panics provoked by economic insecurity, changing family structures, and racial progress. It diverts attention from the underlying causes of the nation's problems and focusses instead on the values and behavior of the poor. Bashing welfare also protects politicians and employers from angry protests by a middle class that is worried about its deteriorating economic situation.

The attack on welfare is also aimed at calming the nation's "moral panic" by projecting fears about society-wide changes in family structures and women's roles onto the poor. Punishing women who do not live in traditional families is a way to ward off challenges to male control posed by single motherhood, as well as by the increased economic independence of women and the expansion of gay and lesbian rights in all income and race groups. The hidden secret about welfare is that *many* women—perhaps even half—turn to AFDC to escape male violence. Indeed, battered women's shelters report that three-quarters of the women they serve use AFDC to establish lives away from batterers.[58] Although social circumstances have changed, patriarchal concepts remain at the center of how families are defined and understood in our culture—we will return to this in Part

3—and penalizing single mothers sends a message to *all* women about what happens to those who do not marry, who raise kids on their own, and who otherwise do not "play by the rules."

Finally, the welfare reformers have turned welfare into a code word for race in order to ease the "racial panic" among white Americans that has arisen as people of color have institutionalized their political and economic gains. Wooing support by pandering to racial fear is not a new phenomenon in U.S. history, but it has certainly had an upsurge since the 1980s. For instance, to incite public hostility to welfare, President Reagan evoked racial stereotypes when he told fictional stories about "welfare queens" who defrauded AFDC and used the money to buy pink Cadillacs. During his 1988 campaign, George Bush splashed pictures of Willie Horton onto TVs across the country in order to indict liberal social programs and tarnish the Democratic candidate for the White House, Michael Dukakis. Horton was an African American who had committed rape and murder while participating in a prison furlough program run by Massachusetts, Dukakis's home state; the presumption was that all prisoners on furlough would act as Willy Horton had. Most recently, Bill Clinton, Newt Gingrich, and many other politicians have tried to enhance their conservative credentials by encouraging the public misperception that almost all women on welfare are black or Latina—when in fact, 40 percent of the AFDC caseload is white. Unable to see past the next election, these officials use racial and ethnic stereotypes to win votes, to protect the wealthy, and to divide people who might join forces and mount a serious challenge to "the system."

In the next chapter we will see that the United States has a long history of blaming welfare for its social and economic problems. As a program for the poor, AFDC has attracted the kind of hostility that was previously directed toward other kinds of relief. And programs for single mothers have a long history of being especially vulnerable to attack. It is to this history that we now turn.

PART 2

A PROGRAM JUST FOR SINGLE MOTHERS

The drive to "reform" welfare is not new: it is simply the most recent in a long series of attacks on programs for the poor, in particular those serving impoverished women. Moreover, neither the target of the attacks nor the rhetoric surrounding them has changed much. This part will look at the history of efforts to reform public assistance: the end of "outdoor relief" in both the early and late 1800s; the creation of Mothers' Pensions in the early 1900s; the inclusion of AFDC as part of the 1935 Social Security Act; the restrictive AFDC policies imposed after World War II; and the crackdown that began in the late 1960s, won a small reprieve, and then continued into the 1980s. From the attack on colonial poor laws to the most recent assault, the critics of welfare have repeatedly targeted women's work and family structures. As with the most recent debate over welfare described in Part 1, in each earlier period welfare came under attack when the provision of relief and the needs of the labor market did not mesh, and when changes in family life threatened the patriarchal status quo.

ATTACKS ON PUBLIC AID
IN THE EARLY NINETEENTH CENTURY

The first major attack on public aid took place in the 1820s, after a thirty-year economic boom and at a time when the Industrial Revolution was leading to vast transformations in work and family patterns. A growing landless population had gathered in the cities and towns, and the proportion of workers employed by others expanded from 12 percent in 1800 to 40 percent in 1860.[1] The emerging urban working class faced a new kind of poverty, one that stemmed less from lack of property, bad harvests, or physical disability than from low wages and irregular work. During this period, although the largest cities increased their per capita spending on the poor, local relief systems could not meet the demand. The indigent included many women: single women who had been "freed" by the decline of household production to labor in the new mills and "manufactories," and the wives of low and irregularly paid men. For example, in 1816, New York City reserved the majority of its relief baskets for women; they were marked with such notations as "husband in prison," "husband has broken leg," "husband bad fellow," and "husband has abandoned her and she has broken her arm."[2]

The existing system of public aid not only began to sag under the weight of the poverty created by the developing market economy, but its methods became both abusive and obsolete. For instance, town officials typically auctioned off the able-bodied poor to the highest bidder, contracted paupers out to local farmers, and barred indigent strangers who might require relief from settling in town. The relief programs relied on aiding people in their own or a neighbor's home and therefore suited an economy based on agricultural production. But because they kept people tied to their households and to the land, the programs interfered with the imperatives of the market economy, which increasingly depended on a mobile and docile labor force rather than independent farmers and artisans. Indeed, the new merchants complained that the poor laws diminished the work effort by "removing the dread of want"—widely held to be the prime mover of the lower orders of society.[3] Nor did the existing system adequately reduce the social turmoil created by wage workers—both men and women—who were beginning to form labor associations and political parties to protect their interests.

The market economy also placed new pressures on family life. For one, the Industrial Revolution and the growth of a waged labor force undercut traditional avenues of upward mobility, which had been based on land ownership, and stimulated travel in search of new opportunities. Such changes loosened family and community ties, weakened paternal control of the home, diminished the family's central role in governing community affairs, and in general discredited traditional social hierarchies and rules of deference. At the same time, social thought increasingly stressed individual self-interest over collective responsibility, respect for privacy over communality, and a sharp gender division of labor based on male breadwinning and female homemaking—all values and attitudes required for successful employment in the market economy.[4] These transformations left the middle class less sure of how to carry out its self-assigned task of imposing standards of personal behavior on the "lower orders." Middle-class social observers became increasingly suspicious of any departure from the new social expectations and critical of the home life of the poor, which they saw as failing to teach moral rectitude and habits of hard work. "Of all the modes of providing for the poor," declared Boston's Mayor Josiah Quincy in the early 1820s, "the most wasteful, the most expensive and the most injurious to their morals and the industrious habits is that of supply in their own families."[5]

The poor law reforms of 1824 therefore were intended to encourage work on the one hand, and remove the poor from their sin-breeding homes on the other. The local authorities began to ban begging, which was how many of the most indigent had been able to survive, and to replace "outdoor" or "home" relief with workhouses and poorhouses, or "indoor" relief (so-named because the poor had to enter institutions in order to receive aid). Arguing that boarding paupers with private families indulged laziness and eroded the deference that should govern class relations, officials refused outdoor relief to any but the "deserving" poor—defined as those who were not married or not working through no fault of their own. They removed the "undeserving" poor from their homes and placed them in institutions that would teach them proper values and insulate them from the temptations of alcohol, gambling, and idleness. One reformer summed up the new policy: "these characters" had to be placed in almshouses where "prohibiting alcohol and mandating work would stimulate their industry and moral feelings."[6]

During the first half of the nineteenth century, therefore, institutionalization became the preferred method of providing for the poor, efforts being strongest in the New England, mid-Atlantic, and mid-western states. As early as 1820, 80 percent of the relief recipients in thirty-one Pennsylvania counties lived in a poorhouse or a workhouse. In New York, the number of almshouses grew from thirty in 1824 to fifty-five in 1857, while the number of inmates soared from 4,500 in 1830 to 10,000 in 1850. Massachusetts, which had 83 such institutions in 1824, had 219 by 1860.[7] The almshouse rapidly deteriorated into a degraded institution that housed the poor alongside criminals, the physically ill, and the insane. Not surprisingly, all but the most desperate were willing to work for any wage or get married to avoid ending up in these institutions. Although the undifferentiated almshouse gradually gave way to hospitals, prisons, orphanages, reformatories, and mental asylums, within fifty years these separate institutions had also deteriorated into little

Residents gather outside an almshouse on Blackwell's (now Roosevelt) Island, New York City, 1890. [Photo by Jacob A. Riis, from the Jacob A. Riis Collection, Museum of the City of New York]

more than custodial warehouses for the poor—many of whom were by this point foreign born.

New explanations of poverty helped justify the shift from outdoor to indoor relief. Early American society had tolerated poverty, which it understood as God's will: the poor deserved the community's help because they could do little to change their station in life and because aiding them in their own or a neighbor's home, or contracting them out to help work the land, seemed both humane and functional. Industrialization challenged this notion: the country's seemingly unlimited natural resources and its sense of great possibility led to the belief that no one who tried hard need be poor, while the new doctrine of individual responsibility held people responsible for their own personal salvation and economic condition. As the growing relief rolls drained the public treasury, critics began to blame poverty on weak moral character; on the taverns, gambling halls, brothels, and other institutions of the new environment that they believed lured the poor into depraved activities; and on the poor laws themselves.

A second attack on relief began in the 1870s, at a time when rapid economic growth was once again creating a set of social problems. Not only did the post-Civil War boom unleash vast amounts of wealth, but the huge influx of immigrants (16 million of the 20 million people who migrated to the United States in the nineteenth century came after 1860) compounded economic inequality because so many of them were poor. Major depressions in the 1870s, 1880s, and 1890s made the situation worse.

The downturn of 1873-1878, sparked by the collapse of the financial and credit markets, put 3 million people out of work and added many people to the relief rolls. To soothe public fears about the rising cost of public aid, the influential New York Association for the Improvement of the Conditions of the Poor (AICP) condemned the poor for shunning work at lowered wages. The AICP also denounced cash aid, free lunches, and public dormitories for catering to "multitudes of the lower and lowest grades of the poor" and "attracting large numbers of tramps and vagrants to the city."[8] The growing hostility to the poor led New York City to suspend outdoor relief between July 1874 and January 1875,[9] leaving 60,000 people without benefits. New York state cut its outdoor relief costs from $976,600 in 1870 to $749,267 in 1880, despite population growth.[10] Boston reduced spending on outdoor public aid from over $80,300 in 1877 to $64,500 in 1900, while Buffalo lowered its expenses from $73,200 in 1875 to $29,300 in 1880. Philadelphia, Baltimore, San Francisco, and St. Louis, among other cities, followed suit. Many women were affected. Although there is little data on the gender distribution of the poor at that time, in 1875 women made up 40 percent of the 11,000 outdoor relief recipients in Philadelphia; 12.5 percent were men and the rest children under age sixteen.[11]

The urban relief rolls also rose during the equally serious downturn of 1882-1885. As in earlier depressions, frantic civic leaders and private charity workers blamed the problem on slipshod relief programs, corrupt politicians, and "ignorant and vicious poor." They also continued to denounce immigration. By 1899, ten of the nation's forty largest cities—home to large numbers of the foreign born—no longer gave outdoor relief, and three others provided very little.[12] As one New York City official put it, it was "better that a few should test the minimum rate [wage] at which existence can be preserved than that the many should find the poorhouse so comfortable a home that they would brave the shame of pauperism to gain admission to it."[13]

Closing relief offices protected the city coffers. It also forced recipients—65 to 75 percent of whom were semi- or unskilled workers—into the labor pool, which helped employers who wanted to replace skilled with unskilled and native-born with foreign-born workers.[14] Industrialists hoped that wage cuts, a longer work day, and the standardization of the labor process through the introduction of machines, supervisors, and simplified work tasks would, together with the greater employment of unskilled labor, increase profits and provide them with greater control of the shop floor.[15] If the pre-Civil War attack on the poor laws had helped to transform a heterogeneous population of farmers and artisans into a waged labor force, the post-

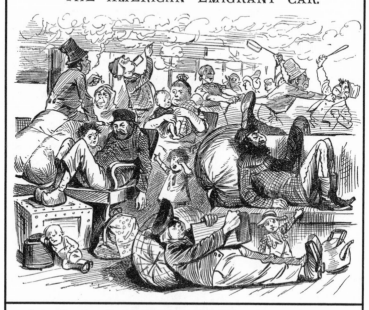

An anti-immigration cartoon from 1882. This catalog of stereotypes includes the Irish with pug noses and wide faces, the Jew with his hook nose and black beard, and, at the center of all the "ruckus," the poor woman with too many babies. [Culver Pictures]

Civil War reforms helped employers deskill the workforce and secure greater power over its labor.

As workers found that they were not sharing in the enormous profits that were accruing to business and industry, a labor movement began to gain strength and fight for a greater piece of the economic pie. Unions increased their membership fourfold between 1880 and 1890, created large federations (such as the International Labor Union and the Knights of Labor), and struck for better wages and working conditions in most of the major industries, including steel, mining, and railroads. Industry, which had formed legal trusts, holding companies, and monopolies in order to consolidate its economic power, fought unionization, hired African Americans and immigrants as scabs, and asked the government to call out the militia to put down strikes. Workers also formed political parties, whose demands ranged from the right to work to the redistribution of the nation's wealth. This upsurge of labor activity fueled attacks on public aid that provided workers with an economic back-up. However small, this assistance which enabled workers to avoid the worst jobs also helped them during strikes and anti-union drives.

Beginning in the early 1870s, newly freed black slaves also lost what little government support was available to them. In 1872, pressure from southern landowners who depended on black sharecroppers led Congress to close down the federally run Freedman's Bureau, which had been created in 1865 to help several million former slaves gain access to education, training, healthcare, and land. In 1877, Congress abandoned all remaining efforts to break down legal inequality in the South, in effect setting in place the marginalization of African-American labor. In 1883, the Supreme Court voided the 1875 Civil Rights Act, ruling that the Fourteenth Amendment did not prohibit discrimination by and against individuals. Many states then quickly passed Jim Crow segregation laws.

The post-Civil War attack on outdoor relief also targeted those who failed to meet the standards of "proper" family life. This time, belief that poor parents were incapable of socializing their children to fit into industrial society and the pressure to break up poor families was reinforced by new explanations of poverty. Social Darwinism and eugenics claimed that wealth was evidence of fitness while destitution signaled inferiority, that behavior patterns could be inherited, and that relief therefore allowed the "unfit" to propagate and survive. The large number of immigrants fueled the eugenics movement, which also equated the unfit with those who were poor, foreign born, and non-white.

Failure to follow middle-class norms thus became a mark of incompetence. Measured against the white, native-born family ideal, the daily features of poor, immigrant, and working-class life—teeming streets, ramshackle tenements without bathtubs, and crowds of children on the stoops—became "evidence" of parental neglect, family disintegration, and a pervasive "pathology." A New York City charity worker described the homes of the poor as "nurseries of indolence, debauchers, and intemperance," and their inhabitants the "moral pests of society."[16] Instead of recognizing these conditions as expected outcomes of life in overcrowded, impoverished communities, they became the antithesis of the proper home and the root of all social evil.

Middle-class reformers were determined to remove poor children from their families. In 1881, for instance, Charles Hoyt, the secretary of the New York State Board of Charities, recommended that parents in need of relief be prepared to cede their natural rights to the state in order "to break the line of pauper descent."[17] The reformers moved poor immigrant children into "American" homes in order to expose them to "truer" and "finer" family culture and to promote assimilation.[18]

The more that mothers were expected to inculcate proper behavior and social norms, the more women were blamed when things went wrong. Poor law officials often removed a child from his or her home because they believed the mother was inadequate to the task of social control. A "deserving widow" might be allowed to keep one or two of her children, but deserted wives, who were often suspected of colluding with their spouses to get aid, were treated more harshly. Officials reserved the severest response for unmarried mothers, however, and they were often forced to enter the workhouse in order to obtain relief.

The policy of breaking up families reached a peak in the last quarter of the nineteenth century, when the mere prospect of disruptiveness was used to justify removing poor children from their homes. Indeed, the line between protecting a family and disciplining it became hopelessly blurred. Not surprisingly, the number of children placed in orphanages skyrocketed, not only because of court mandates but because many parents had no choice but to place their children in institutions if they were to save them from starvation. By the end of the century, the relief rolls had been reduced, but poverty had also deepened.

CREATING A PROGRAM FOR SINGLE MOTHERS

By the early 1900s, 5.3 million women, or 20 percent of all women, were working for wages outside the home.[19] Some reformers feared that women took jobs away from men and that their working challenged gender norms—even though most occupations remained sex-segregated. They also worried about the large number of children warehoused in orphanages because their single mothers could not support them or because women worked long hours and had no other source of childcare. And finally, the reformers feared that when poverty forced single mothers to work outside the home, the children who were left unsupervised might become delinquent, and would in any case not be properly prepared for "citizenship." The future of the nation, they argued, depended on proper upbringing by quality mothers in the home. It was these considerations that led to the campaign for Mothers' Pensions, which became the forerunner of AFDC.

The idea of Mothers' Pensions arose during the Progressive Era (1896-1914), a time when both middle-class reformers *and* the heads of some of the largest corporations wanted more government management of the increasingly complex and volatile economy. Spearheaded by women, the campaign for Mothers' Pensions sought greater government responsibility for the well-being of all poor women and children, but especially widows, who in 1900 headed 77 percent of all mother-only families.[20] Another 16 percent were headed by deserted wives, very few of whom got legal divorces. Unmarried motherhood, rare but on the rise, was more common in black than white households. To avoid public reproach, both deserted wives and single mothers often called themselves widows.

The advocates of Mothers' Pensions therefore focussed on widows and billed the pension as a grant for the special services which these mothers provided and which were necessary for the welfare of the children and the community. By singling out widows, they were able to defang the criticism of those who condemned aid to "immoral" women, and they emphasized that the pension was a payment for the services of motherhood in order to avoid the stigma attached to the traditional "dole." Not surprisingly, then, the "worthy" mothers were more likely to be not only widowed but native-born and white.

However, even "deserving" widows—referred to as "gilt-edged" by some commentators—did not totally escape censure. In exchange for economic support, public officials subjected them to restrictions intended to make sure they conformed to prescribed gender and cultural norms. Agency investigators monitored the women closely for signs of drinking, lax spending, unkempt homes, improper childrearing practices, and relationships with men. They urged foreign-born women to take English and civics classes, cook American dishes, and otherwise conform to white middle-class ways. Middle-class reformers generally accepted the view that immigrants were socially inferior to Anglo Saxons and that poverty was an index of cultural inferiority, although they rejected the biological determinism of nativists and racists. They believed that racial and cultural differences could be transcended and made Mothers' Pensions their instrument for assimilation.

Between 1911 and 1921, forty states enacted Mothers' Pensions, and by 1932 the program existed in all but two states (but not in every county). The pension improved the lives of many poor women and children, but because it stigmatized poor women and welfare, in the long run it opened both to attack. The glorification of Anglo-American motherhood, the belief in childrearing as exclusively women's work, the narrow vision of proper single mothers as widows, and the identification of worthiness with assimilation condemned other mothers who did not live up to these ideals as immoral and unworthy of aid.

Mothers' Pensions also perpetuated the poor law, or charity, model of public assistance: low benefits, sporadic implementation, and emphasis on moral reform. While quieting opposition from private charities that feared competition from public

A "White Plague" (tuberculosis) poster being shown to Italians in their home, 1908. [Photo by Byron, from the Byron Collection, Museum of the City of New York]

programs and from local officials who worried about state control, these features limited the value of Mothers' Pensions for poor women. The alternatives that were rejected at the time—programs that would serve *all* children, *all* poor women as compensation for their caretaking work, and *both* single and two-parent families (through a family allowance)—assumed that public aid was a right rather than a privilege. Many proponents of these broader programs nevertheless supported Mothers' Pensions, hoping that they would open the door to a larger future role for the government. Had any of the alternatives been accepted, however, programs serving poor families would most likely have been considerably less vulnerable to attack.

THE SOCIAL SECURITY ACT: FROM MOTHERS' PENSIONS TO ADC

The Mothers' Pension program and its philosophy of moral reform were incorporated into the 1935 Social Security Act as Aid to Dependent Children (ADC). While the landmark Social Security Act modernized the social welfare system by, among other things, transferring responsibility for social welfare from the states to the federal government, the gender politics of the period meant that the treatment of women, and particularly of unmarried mothers, remained steadfastly traditional.[21]

The mostly male architects of the Social Security Act hoped to insure white, male industrial workers against labor market risks through such measures as unemployment compensation and social security retirement benefits. They displayed little interest in the needs of women, other than as wives of workers. At the same time, the women reformers—the only people with influence in social security circles who were also concerned about poor single women—remained committed to the Mothers' Pension ideal. These women believed that the Mothers' Pension model would serve single mothers better than the employment-based Social Security schemes favored by the planners of the Act. Few in either group believed that Mothers' Pensions would be a source of independence for women.

Officially known as Title IV of the 1935 Social Security Act, Aid to Dependent Children honored motherhood in principle but regulated mothers in practice, and was quite limited in a number of ways. First, Congress rejected a definition of "dependent children" that would have entitled any poor child to assistance as long as the family breadwinner could not work or provide a reasonable subsistence. This interpretation would have allowed the government to aid children living with single parents and children in two-parent homes with unemployed and underemployed fathers, as well as children who were staying with relatives or living in foster homes. In sharp contrast, due in part to strong pressure from employers of cheap labor, especially in the South, who wanted to maintain existing patterns of economic exploitation and racial domination, the final legislation offered assistance only to children deprived of parental support due to the death, continued absence, or incapacity of the family breadwinner.

In addition to limiting ADC to single mothers, Congress rejected proposals to make its benefits compatible with "decency and health." Instead, the grant was capped at $18 per month for the first child and $12 for each additional child. No money was included for a child's caretaker (this did not change until 1950). In contrast, the same legislation provided a maximum of $30 a month for adults receiving Old Age Assistance (OAA) and Aid to the Blind (AB), even though these recipients were not as likely to have children in the home. ADC rules not only forced many mothers into the labor force, but required applicants to pass a demeaning means test to "prove" their lack of income and resources. Congress eventually added this income test to all the public assistance programs. In addition, although the states could set their own benefit levels, few reached the recommended federal maximum. The southern states rationalized their lower-than-average grants by declaring that black families needed less than white families did.

There was also less federal reimbursement for ADC than for the other public assistance programs. Congress provided $1 for every dollar spent by the states on the aged and blind, but only $1 for every $2 spent on dependent children. In 1936, federal expenditures accounted for 43 percent of the Old Age Assistance program, 22 percent of the Aid to the Blind program, and 13 percent of the ADC program. Not surprisingly, state implementation of ADC lagged far behind that of the other programs—so that by the end of 1936, OAA existed in forty-two states and ADC in only twenty-six. By 1940, two-thirds of all eligible children remained uncovered—despite the fact that the ADC caseload had doubled since 1936.

The ADC program perpetuated the Mothers' Pension practice of using public aid to enforce behavioral standards. Both programs categorized women as "deserving" and "undeserving" based on their compliance with traditional marital and family arrangements. But although *all* the Social Security Act programs penalized husbandless women (other than widows), the ADC methods were especially harsh. Shortly after the act's passage and in the name of raising the standards of family life, the Social Security Board called for home visits and periodic eligibility checks. It encouraged the states to make aid contingent on the maintenance of a "suitable" home, which was defined in terms of the mother's sexual, childbearing, and parenting behavior. Signs of a male presence or the birth of an "illegitimate" child could disqualify a family—making ADC the only public assistance program to impose a morals test on its applicants.

Despite its severe limitations, the ADC program did improve public aid for poor single mothers. First, making ADC and the other public assistance programs federal-state partnerships enlarged federal responsibility for social welfare. Although the states were allowed to set their own eligibility rules and benefit levels, federal oversight led to some national standards and limits on the discretionary power and discriminatory practices of local welfare offices. Perhaps most important, the guarantee of federal matching funds created an entitlement to public aid.

Congress amended the Social Security Act in 1939. The amendments were designed to make Old Age Insurance (OAI) stronger than the public assistance program serving the aged poor (Old Age Assistance, or OAA) by moving up its starting date and by adding special benefits for a deceased worker's surviving dependent widow and children (whether or not the wife herself worked for wages).[22] The transfer of widows from ADC to Social Security further institutionalized ADC as a program just for "undeserving" poor women. For one, the shift further hardened distinctions among women based on marital status. And second, left to serve only the socially unacceptable divorced, separated, and never-married single mothers, ADC grew increasingly stigmatized. The amendments also deepened the act's racial divide: since many black men did not qualify for social security benefits at all, *their* widows and children could not receive OAI (which was twice what children received on ADC); needy women of color thus had no choice but to apply for assistance.[23] At the same time, the transfer of white widows to

OAI ensured that in the future nonwidowed and nonwhite single mothers would become overrepresented on ADC, leaving the program open to hostility from a public that continued to denigrate the poor, women, and people of color.

THE POSTWAR ATTACK, 1945-1960

The welfare state expanded rapidly after World War II, fueled by population growth, postwar prosperity, the liberalization of existing programs, a greater sense of public responsibility for social problems, the ability of the nation to meet the needs of the poor more adequately, and demands for greater economic security from both the trade union and civil rights movements. During the postwar boom, Congress extended social insurance coverage to some (but not all) of the farm, domestic, and self-employed workers who had been left out of the original act. It added cash assistance for ADC mothers in 1950 and benefits for disabled workers in 1956. Congress also enacted a national School Lunch Program (1946), the Mental Health Act (1946), the Hill-Burton Hospital Construction Act (1946), the Employment Act (1946), the Housing Act (1949), the School Milk Program (1954), and the Vocational Rehabilitation Act (1954). This growing social welfare system was designed to protect the unprotected against what were increasingly seen as the uncontrollable risks faced by individuals and families living and working in an industrial society. They also benefitted many middle-class families and not a few corporations, which depended on these programs to ensure consumer buying power, to keep the workforce healthy and educated, and in general to maintain the social peace.

The expansion and liberalization of the welfare state during the late 1940s and early 1950s did not go uncontested. While advocates continued to press for improvements, opponents in and outside of the Republican Congress argued that the welfare state represented "big government" and "creeping socialism." Fueled by postwar anti-communism and rising conservatism, ADC in particular was attacked by the Eisenhower administration and by many governors, even though it was not by any means the largest or most expensive welfare program. The hostility was fueled by regular press reports proclaiming that the ADC rolls had risen from 372,000 in 1940 to 803,000 in 1960, while spending had jumped from $130 million in 1940 to $550 million in 1950 to $995 million in 1960.[24] However, the press failed to note that during these twenty years the number of women on welfare fluctuated with changes in social and economic conditions. Between 1936 and 1940, the Depression and ADC's start-up enrollments raised the rolls from 162,000 to 372,000 families. The numbers fell during World War II, due to the increased demand for female labor. Between 1945 and 1950, wages and salaries rose 23 percent, but inflation and unemployment also took a toll, so that in 1950 one-fifth of the population lived in poverty.[25] Prices continued to rise even during the first postwar economic slump, which began in 1949, and unemployment grew steadily, abating only when the Korean war provided a brief economic stimulus. Welfare rolls declined during the war but increased again during the recessions of 1953-1954 and 1957-1958. By 1960, 20 percent of all whites, nearly 50 percent of people living in female-headed households, and more than half of all African Americans were poor, so the rolls began to rise again.[26]

The attack on welfare was fueled by anxieties about public spending that arose when the government introduced a payroll deduction system that transformed the income tax from a class tax (a tax on the top income groups) to a mass tax (one that affected nearly all workers). By 1943, 40 million people from all social classes were paying federal income taxes, up from only 4 million (mostly affluent) people in 1939.[27] This happened at the same time that more was being spent on ADC. As a result, by the 1950s the white middle class was more than ready to scapegoat those receiving public aid.

Ignoring the clear link between lower wages, fewer jobs, economic recession, and the increased number of women applying for ADC, politicians and the media attacked the program. From the early 1940s to the 1960s, critics cut benefits, stiffened eligibility rules, investigated local welfare departments for fraud, and otherwise tried to keep women off the rolls. As in earlier periods, they blamed the expansion of ADC not on the economy but on the behavior of poor women and the availability of relief. As a New York City domestic relations court judge told reporters, "The relief set up is sapping the will to work, encouraging cynicism and petty chiseling." The popular news magazines revived negative stereotypes of welfare mothers as "lazy" and "immoral," and painted lurid pictures of welfare recipients as women who spent money on maids, TV sets, cars, and jewelry. The headline of one popular mass-circulation magazine declared: "Want $3680 a year, tax free? You are required only to have no self-respect and never get a job. Buy all the liquor you want ... and the welfare department will help you."[28]

Welfare, Women's Work, and the Labor Market

The anti-welfare rhetoric masked one of the underlying reasons for the attack on ADC: the competing demand for women's unpaid labor in the home and their low-paid labor in the market. This chronic tension intensified during the postwar years because the occupations that relied heavily on female workers were expanding while demographic shifts and postwar attitudes toward women's work were shrinking the pool of women who might have filled these jobs.

To begin with, the female labor force was not growing fast enough to meet the demand. The number of women who typically worked outside the home—older widowed and divorced women—remained stable, while low prewar birth rates and high postwar marriage rates reduced the supply of young single women available for work. Since older married white women with grown children were already working in large numbers, they could not fill the gap. Racism made employers reluctant to hire African-American women, who had always worked outside the home, in these new and better jobs.

The growing demand for women workers also conflicted with widespread fears that there would not be enough jobs for the returning soldiers. While ending war-related production freed several hundred thousand women up for other jobs,[29] many of them withdrew from the labor force because of the strains of combining housekeeping with paid employment and in response to the postwar campaign to send women back into the home. The mass media told women it was their patriotic duty to give up their jobs to returning soldiers, maligned employed women as un-feminine "Amazons" who could outdrink, outswear, and outswagger men, and popularized social science research which proclaimed that working wives created marital friction, family instability, and neurotic children.[30] By 1950 there was a net drop in the rate at which married mothers aged twenty-five to thirty-four with young children were going to work.[31] The Women's Bureau, by 1953, was reporting severe shortages of typists, stenographers, nurses, teachers, social workers, and medical aides.[32] The GI Bill exacerbated overall labor shortages by enabling millions of returning veterans to attend college instead of entering the labor market.

Working-class women who could not afford to stay home met some of the demand, but rather than keeping their higher paying wartime jobs in industry, they were bumped into lower paying "women's" jobs. The demand for women workers eventually helped black women to win higher wages in domestic work, or even to avoid it altogether, but this in turn created panic among white middle-class housewives, and lead the Women's Bureau to develop programs to train black women for "service." By 1950, 60 percent of black women, but only 16 percent of white women, worked in private households or institutional service jobs.[33]

African Americans who were dislocated by the mechanization of southern agriculture and women on welfare were two additional sources of labor. In the late 1940s and 1950s, many states forced women to work by lowering ADC benefits and restricting access to the program.[34] Officials publicized the names of recipients to deter people from seeking aid. To weed out suspected "frauds" and to otherwise harass recipients, some welfare departments closed out entire caseloads and then required everyone to reapply, hoping that many would not want to undergo another eligibility investigation. In the early 1950s, after the Eisenhower administration pressed for greater local control of welfare, state after state added punitive administrative policies in order to remove recipients from the rolls and slow new applications. In states that did not actively deny women benefits or require that they work part-time, welfare departments made sure that those receiving aid were less well-off than those who were working by subtracting one ADC dollar for every dollar earned.

The effort to enlarge the labor pool by restricting welfare was especially intense in the South.[35] From the days of slavery, white society had valued African-American women as workers and denied them the protection and rights of womanhood granted to white women. During the 1940s and 1950s, southern states intentionally restricted welfare in order to force black women to work. In 1943, Louisiana refused aid to mothers with young children who appeared "employable," especially during the harvest season. In 1952, Georgia directed local welfare boards to deny all applications (and close all cases) of employable mothers in "periods of full employment," that is, when they were needed in the cotton and tobacco fields; a similar "farm policy" was adopted in Arkansas in 1953. In 1954, a Louisiana civic leader explicitly complained that "public assistance results in reducing the unskilled labor ... in employment where women and children form a principal part of the supply." Southern employers believed there was "no reason why the employable Negro mother should not continue her usually sketchy seasonal labor or indefinite domestic service rather than receive a public assistance grant," and many local welfare departments gave black women less money than they did to white women. In addition, the strict enforcement of year-long state residency requirements prevented many African-American women (as well as southwestern Latina migrants) from receiving aid. A nationwide study conducted by the Department of Health, Education, and Welfare in 1961 reported that 19 percent of black mothers on welfare worked, compared to only 10 percent of white mothers on welfare, and most of those who were working lived in the South.[36]

Forcing women on welfare to work not only helped fill jobs at the bottom rungs of the employment ladder in the expanding service sector, but also reproduced and enforced patterns of racial domination during a period of growing racial tension and militant protest. The increased competition between blacks and whites for jobs and housing contributed to a wave of anti-black violence in 1944, including major conflagrations in Detroit, Michigan; Harlem, New York; Mobile, Alabama; and Beaumont, Texas. Black workers won a ban against discrimination in defense production (1941), the elimination of the all-white primary (1944), and presidential support for desegregating the military (1948). In the mid-1950s, emboldened by the 1954 Supreme Court ban on separate-but-equal schools, the civil rights movement shed its original "go slow" strategy and launched an all-out attack on segregation. In 1955, blacks organized the Montgomery Bus Boycott. In August 1957, Congress passed the first Civil Rights Act in eighty-two years; in September the President sent troops to Arkansas so that black students could enter Central High School. As we will see in Part 4, southern black women formed the backbone of the ensuing boycotts, mass demonstrations, civil disobedience, and voter registration drives. Blacks, including women, had become "uppity" and had to be "put in their place."

Women, Welfare, and the Family

In their effort to reduce the rolls, the postwar welfare critics also targeted poor women's marital and childbearing patterns. The rising demand for women workers challenged women's traditional relationship to the family by reducing their economic dependence on men. So did the "epidemic" of marital break-ups and out-of-wedlock births which resulted from hasty wartime unions, the stress of wartime separations, as well as greater self-reliance on the part of women who had lived alone and/or earned their own incomes during the war. The divorce rate climbed from 16 per 100 marriages in 1940 to 25 per 100 in 1950 (more, if separations are included). Nonmarital births among women aged fifteen to forty-four tripled between 1940 and 1960, rising from 7.1 to 21.6 per 1,000 women. The rate for white women jumped from 3.6 to 9.2 per 1,000; the rate for black women, which was already much higher, increased somewhat more slowly, from 35.6 to 98.3 per 1,000.[37]

The high rates of marital break-ups and non-marital births among blacks stemmed in part from wartime dislocations, but also from persistent black male unemployment and the strains of both racism and poverty. On the other hand, the black community showed a greater willingness to sustain women on their own, to respect women's employment, and to share child raising among extended networks of kin.[38]

The changes in family structure among women in all walks of life heightened concerns about what we today call "family values" and led to a panic about the breakdown of the family and the "proper" role for women. This in turn fueled the attack on ADC. Social scientists, policymakers, and mental health professionals raised questions about the ability of working women to raise children and blamed truancy, running away, juvenile delinquency, and almost every other personal and social problem on mothers—underinvolved or overinvolved white mothers and overbearing or emasculating black matriarchs. Public concern about these issues was projected onto poor women and the ADC program. The experts reported that poor "hard-to-reach" families—many headed by women—were the breeding ground for social problems and absorbed most of the social welfare resources.[39] The criticism of single mothers extended to the ADC program which, reflecting both the transfer of widows to the Social Security program and changing family patterns in wider society, now served many fewer widows and many more divorced, separated, and never-married women, all of whom were still considered immoral and undeserving of aid.[40]

The assault on ADC was compounded by the dramatic postwar change in the racial composition of the welfare rolls. Before World War II, black women comprised between 14 and

17 percent of all women on ADC—a number that would have been higher if welfare departments had not discriminated against them. After the war, the black portion of the ADC caseload grew rapidly, from 21 percent in 1942 to 30 percent in 1948 to 48 percent in 1961.[41] As this occurred, the animosity surrounding public assistance shifted its focus from immigrants to blacks, and the justification for cutting aid changed from preserving the "purity of the native stock" to evoking racial stereotypes of black women as promiscuous, matriarchal, and welfare-dependent. The racial tensions were apparent in newspaper headlines: "It Pays to Play the Pauper," read one headline in *Nation's Business* in 1950. Another proclaimed that "Relief Is Ruining Families." A 1961 article in *Look* magazine, entitled "Welfare: Has It Become Scandal?" complained that "relief ... had spawned a vicious cycle in welfare so that now a second generation is maturing on the welfare rolls. The girls [in these families] take their pregnancies as a matter of course. The home is like Grand Central Terminal.... All the girls should have been put in homes."[42]

The federal and state governments responded to this public barrage by penalizing women for their marital and childbearing choices.[43] Much of the anti-welfare activity took the form of "substitute father" and "man-in-the-house" rules designed to force men into paying child support, to prevent them from living off a women's welfare check, and to enforce sexual norms. Some states penalized a woman for having a relationship with a man who did not have a blood relationship to her children. In 1950, for instance, South Carolina concluded that children were not "deprived" of parental support if there was "any man with whom the mother had a common-law relationship, even if he did not stay in the home regularly or support the children." Alabama reduced its rolls by 25 percent by cutting women who were "going with a man," Arkansas denied aid to mothers engaged in a "non-stable, non-legal union," Michigan to families with male "borders," and Texas to "pseudo-common law" marriages. To enforce these regulations, welfare investigators pried into the private lives of recipients, in many cases conducting midnight raids "to catch men visiting overnight in welfare homes."

By 1950 more than half the states had also passed "suitable home" laws that limited aid to "fit" mothers.[44] In 1951, the governor of Georgia declared that he was "willing to tolerate an unwed mother who makes one mistake, but not when the mistake is repeated three, four, or five times." His welfare department denied aid to children born to unwed women on the rolls. In 1960, as part of a package "to counteract racial integration," Louisiana made it a crime to have more than one "illegitimate" child and struck more than 20,000 children from the program. In 1961, Newburgh, New York, imposed time limits on ADC, removed children from "unsuitable homes," and cut the benefits for unwed ADC mothers who had additional children while receiving aid. North Carolina officials went even as far as discussing the sterilization of ADC women to reduce their costs!

THE WELFARE CRISIS AND WELFARE REFORM, 1967-1972

The second major attack on welfare in the twentieth century took place at the end of the 1960s. The welfare rolls had grown dramatically during this decade (and especially after 1964), particularly in urban centers in the North and the West. The number of families receiving ADC rose from 803,000 in 1960 to about 1 million in 1965 and then shot up to 1.9 million in 1970 and to just under 3 million in 1972. Benefit payments increased from $995 million in 1960 to $7 billion in 1972. Moreover, the numbers climbed steadily even when conditions improved—during the Vietnam War, for instance—and despite a drop in the poverty rate, from 22 percent of the population in 1960 to 12 percent in 1972.[45]

What the press called the welfare "explosion" was in fact the result of a complex set of social, economic, and political forces. First, the continued growth of the population, of families headed by women, and of poor families swelled the rolls. By 1969, 24 million people lived in poverty, and the wages of many workers were no longer keeping pace with the rising cost of living. The liberalization of welfare policy had also played a role. In 1961, Congress raised the ADC need standard. The 1962 Social Security Act amendments allowed women on welfare to work and collect benefits, permitted the states to provide services to a broad range of current and potential recipients, made a limited group of two-parent households eligible for aid—it was at this point that the name was changed from ADC to Aid to Families with Dependent Children, or AFDC.

Finally, political pressures contributed to the expansion of AFDC. The growing strength of the civil rights movement in the North, the massive March on Washington in 1963, the 1964 and 1968 uprisings by large numbers of marginalized African Americans, and the emergence of the black power movement forced the Democratic Party to support both civil rights and social welfare legislation.[46] The push to reform welfare was furthered by the organization of thousands of welfare mothers into the highly effective National Welfare Rights Union (NWRO) which brought attention to the plight of poor women and fear of more disorder into the hearts of local civic and business leaders (we will return to this period in Part 4).

Since the majority of African Americans in the North lived in a few large cities in states with many electoral votes, politicians began to worry that they had the votes to swing presidential elections. Some blacks had already threatened to bolt the Democratic Party to protest its sluggish civil rights record. Hoping to hold onto its black constituents, to mute civil rights protests, and to prevent more ghetto uprisings, the liberal wing of the party engineered the passage of the Civil Rights Act (1964), the Voting Rights Act (1965), and Medicaid and Medicare (1965). In 1964, the Democrats also launched a "war on poverty," which promoted the "maximum feasible participation" of the poor in civic affairs and funded city agencies to develop new healthcare, childcare, employment, and legal services. Congress extended AFDC to children between the ages of eighteen and twenty-one who were still attending school (1964) and to children in foster care (1969), and raised the standard of need (1969). By 1970, the Supreme Court had invalidated restrictive residency requirements, the intrusive "man-in-the-house" rules, and the onerous "substitute-father" regulations.

Not surprisingly, the proportion of applicants accepted for AFDC jumped, from 62 percent in 1965 to 74 percent in 1969. And once state barriers dropped, the program served even more unmarried women, while the proportion of blacks rose slightly, from 46 in 1961 to a peak of 49 percent in 1967. The value of welfare benefits increased by 36 percent from 1965 to 1970, compared to a 27 percent increase from 1955 to 1960 and a 19 percent increase from 1950 to 1955. Since only half of all eligible women actually applied for AFDC, experts fearfully predicted that the rolls would rise even farther and that federal AFDC costs would increase, possibly reaching $1.84 billion by 1972.[47] By the late 1960s, many politicians and social analysts were arguing that the program had become too large and costly and needed to be "reformed."

As in the past, two underlying issues loomed large in the ensuing attack: the relationship between welfare and the labor market, and the relationship between welfare and family life. But the particulars that sparked the attack were different: this time, instead of labor shortages, the main problem was that welfare benefits had begun to exceed wages. In addition, never-married, rather than previously married, women were increasingly appearing on the rolls.

Low Wages and Labor Shortages

In the late 1960s, welfare critics began to argue that AFDC had become more attractive than work. For instance, in his 1967 inaugural address as governor of California, Ronald Reagan declared, "We are not going to perpetuate poverty by substituting a permanent dole for a paycheck. There is no humanity in destroying self-reliance, dignity and self-respect—the very substance of moral fiber." Wilbur Mills, chair of the House Ways and Means Committee, asked, "Is it in the public interest for welfare to become a way of life?" In late 1965, a Chicago cab driver expressed a widespread point of view: "The goddamn people sit around when they should be working and they're having illegitimate kids to get more money. You know their morals are different. They don't give a damn."[48]

The pressure to retrench welfare reflected more than growing costs or a backlash against nonwhite recipients, however. It also reflected a feeling that AFDC no longer regulated the workforce effectively. A change in the relationship between wages and welfare benefits in high-benefit states made AFDC more economically attractive than full-time work, and this in turn made it harder for AFDC rules to force women into the labor force when needed. Between 1947 and 1962, both ADC payments and wages rose by two-thirds, but because they rose in tandem, the smaller ADC grant remained below the market wage. In sharp contrast, between 1960 and 1970, the average earnings of workers rose by 48 percent, while the average AFDC benefits jumped 75 percent. In the early 1970s, the AFDC grant exceeded the minimum wage in many high-benefit states.[49] Even though it did this by only a small amount, welfare became an economically rational choice for some poor women.

This shift in the relationship between welfare and wages violated a fundamental rule of public assistance: that its benefits remain below the lowest prevailing wage to ensure that only the most desperate will choose it over work. The shift also made it harder to move AFDC mothers in and out of the workforce on an as-needed basis, much less to channel them permanently into the labor market. Economists and politicians blamed the rising rolls on "high" benefits instead of low wages and worried that, if left unchanged, AFDC would erode the work ethic, reduce the labor supply, and, in the prevailing tight labor market, force wages up. Rather than raise wages for all women, the experts decided to make work a requirement for receiving AFDC.

Until this time, federal AFDC rules had prohibited women on welfare from working; this had been enforced by charging any casual earnings against the relief grant (so a women who combined welfare and part-time work would not be better off than a women working for wages full time). As described above, many states tried to sidestep these procedures, and when the federal government clamped down, they found other ways to limit access: Arizona passed a closed-end appropriation to reduce funding if the AFDC program grew bigger than the budget; Connecticut instituted a flat-grant system that eliminated payment for special needs; Kansas cut AFDC benefits 20 percent across the board; Maine eliminated AFDC for unemployed fathers (AFDC-UP); New Jersey replaced AFDC-UP with assistance to the working poor that paid two-thirds of the AFDC standard; Nebraska cut payments 10 percent; Texas cut its maximum payment for a family from $135 to $125 a month—and so on.

In 1962, Congress also attempted to get welfare mothers to work by using such incentives as training and social services to increase their employability. But this "rehabilitation" or "social service" strategy did not reduce the welfare rolls quickly enough. Instead of waiting for longer term outcomes, impatient legislators, led by Wilbur Mills, cracked down and included a tough work program, called the Work Incentive Program (WIN) as part of the 1967 amendments to the Social Security Act.[50] WIN required women on welfare to find work or to register for some kind of employment and training program. Although mothers receiving AFDC could keep part of their earnings while receiving the full welfare grant, WIN was nevertheless coercive: for the first time in the history of the program, any mother with children over the age of 6 had to work or participate in a job-training or work program in order to receive a grant. If she refused she risked losing her welfare check. WIN was followed in 1971 by the Talmadge Amendment, or WIN II, which further stiffened work requirements, scuttled WIN's job-training programs, and strengthened sanctions for noncompliance, including penalties for states that failed to enroll enough recipients into the program.

WIN II's budget grew to more than $300 million in 1974 (where it remained until 1981, when it began to decline), but enrollment fell below expectations. For one, welfare department staff could not handle all the new registrants. Moreover, federal rules exempted sick and disabled women from the work requirements, as well as mothers who were needed at home to care for young children or who had no childcare services available. (It is important to note here that within welfare circles, many still believed that women belonged at home.) The program also ignored the fact that low earnings enabled WIN participants to work and still qualify for some AFDC benefits, and that many AFDC recipients already combined welfare and work. The ambivalence about sending women to work, as well as outright sex discrimination, also led WIN workers to place more welfare fathers (from the small AFDC-UP program) than mothers in the WIN work programs. Whites, who made up less than half of the AFDC caseload, received far more than half of the available job placements.

WIN II remained in place until it was superseded by JOBS, the work program that was part of the 1988 Family Support Act (described in Part 1). Despite its limitations, WIN processed 800,000 recipients a year. While not everyone ended up with a job, the employment of women on welfare increased by 25 percent or more in fifteen states, 50 percent or more in nine states, and over 100 percent in three states. At the same time, WIN's combination of harsh rules and strict work incentives added to the low-wage labor supply by channeling thousands of AFDC mothers into low-paid jobs and by deterring unknown numbers of women from applying for aid in the first place. By increasing the size of the labor pool, WIN also helped to keep wages down, in effect subsidizing low-wage employers, instead of pressing them to make work more attractive than welfare by raising wages.

A Woman's Right to Choose

The attack on welfare in the late 1960s and early 1970s also targeted women's social and sexual autonomy. In the 1960s, large numbers of people became alarmed about relaxed sexual norms (casual sex, easier divorces, increased cohabitation), changing family structures (falling birth rates, later marriages, more middle-class single mothers), and a permissive youth culture (college dropouts, drug use, singles' bars).

The trend toward women and children living on their own was continuing: in the 1960s, one in twenty unmarried women had a child; by 1970, the number had jumped to one in ten. Further, the numbers understated the extent of change since they excluded many pregnant women who married, shotgun or not, before their children were born. The growth of AFDC reflected these wider societal trends,[51] as well as the activities of the National Welfare Rights Organization, the War on Poverty, and the public debate about reforming public assistance, all of which made more single mothers aware of the availability of AFDC. However, instead of acknowledging that the growth of never-married single mothers on AFDC stemmed even in part from these trends, the welfare critics put unwed mothers on AFDC forward as the prime example of a growing danger: the decline in family stability.

In addition, the women's movement made patriarchy and sexism public issues for the first time since the early 1900s. Calls for reproductive freedom, equal employment rights, and the end of male control of women's lives, as well as a spotlight on rape, incest, and battering, awakened large numbers of middle-class women to gender oppression on the job and at home. Welfare provided women with an alternative to such oppression, however limited, and appeared to endorse the idea that women could choose among depending on men (marriage), the labor market, or the state for economic support. Although only poor and working-class women could apply for AFDC, and although many did not actually take up the opportunity, the availability of welfare seemed to permit more female autonomy than the wider society was prepared to grant. To make matters worse, by the end of the decade the patriarchal underpinnings of welfare had also become part of a welfare rights critique. In her path-breaking 1972 article, "Welfare Is a Women's Issue," Johnnie

Tillmon, president of the National Welfare Rights Organization, linked the concerns of poor and middle-class women as follows:

> There are a lot of other lies that male society tells about welfare mothers: that AFDC mothers are immoral, that AFDC mothers are lazy, misuse their welfare checks, spend it all on booze and are stupid and incompetent. If people are willing to believe these lies, it's partly because they are just special versions of the lies that society tells about all women. For instance, the notion that AFDC mothers are lazy: that's just a negative version of the idea that women don't work and don't want to. It's a way of rationalizing the male policy of keeping women as domestic slaves. The notion that AFDC mothers are immoral is another way of saying that all women are likely to become whores unless they're kept under control by men and marriage.[52]

In addition to maligning women on welfare as lazy, the attack on welfare, as Tillmon pointed out, reflected public anxieties about the growing personal and sexual autonomy of women.

Translating fears of female autonomy into concerns about "proper" motherhood, the welfare critics attacked the right of poor women to bear children on their own. In 1966, when Congress modified the Social Security Act to allow the states to move children into foster care if their home environments were poor, "illegitimacy" was chosen as the main indicator of this condition. The 1967 Amendments froze federal funds for AFDC cases that could be attributed to desertion or nonmarital births, but maintained funding for "properly" married women—widowed AFDC mothers and wives in AFDC-UP households. Driven by the unsubstantiated view that women in poverty deliberately have children to increase their welfare grants, these federal rules penalized the states for any increase in the proportion of "illegitimate" children in their AFDC caseloads. Congress never implemented (and eventually repealed) the freeze, but only after two years of pressure from the social service establishment, civil rights organizations, and the welfare rights movement. Nevertheless, the assault continued at the local level. In 1971, a Tennessee legislator introduced a bill to sterilize unwed mothers who applied for welfare on pain of losing custody of their children. In 1972, a California welfare advisory board proposed that any woman who had a third nonmarital child should be declared unfit and be forced to hand the third child over to the state. Similar rules to limit women's right to choose also went into effect in other states.[53]

Black women again took the brunt of the attack. For instance, Julius Horowitz, writing for *New York Times Magazine* in 1965, implied that black single mothers lacked maternal commitment when he wrote, "We know that the damage to the infant takes place long before he [sic] sees the dirt, the drunks, the drug addicts, the spilled garbage of the slum; the damage takes place when the unavailable mother brings her child home from the hospital and realizes she hates him for being alive."[54] Daniel Patrick Moynihan's controversial report, *The Negro Family* (1965), focused on welfare, delinquency, unemployment, drug addiction, and school failure in the black community, concluding that its social problems were unique and stemmed almost exclusively from the "breakdown" of the family.[55] Moynihan ignored both the strengths of the black family and the impact of poverty and racial inequality on its well-being, and overestimated the differences between poor black and poor white families.

STILL MORE WELFARE REFORM

The attack on poor women as lazy and immoral continued during the 1970s, as did WIN's work requirements—even though the AFDC caseload had stabilized at about 3.5 million families. Meanwhile, the falling standard of living among two-parent working-class households began to create problems for both political parties. In 1968, thousands of disaffected white Democrats voted Republican. Both parties felt the need to win these voters over. This led Nixon, in his Family Assistance Plan (1971), and Carter, in his Better Jobs and Income Program (1976), to propose extending welfare to two-parent families headed by men. Both legislative initiatives failed. They also tried to create jobs through the Public Employment Program (PEP, 1970) and the Comprehensive Employment and Training Program (CETA, 1971); and to provide income support through the Earned Income Tax Credit (1976) and a job-tax credit that subsidized employers. There were also proposals to nationalize welfare, to improve income-conditioned housing subsidies, to establish a Basic Opportunity Grant for college students, and to liberalize tax deductions for childcare. There were no proposals, however, for raising the minimum wage.

The effort to use welfare, job creation, and tax credits to improve the economic situation of two-parent working-class families contrasted sharply with the historically harsh assaults on families headed by women and was short-lived. President Reagan began his drastic budget cuts in 1981, and, as we saw in Part 1, in the mid-1980s launched another drive to reform welfare for single mothers. This led to the Family Support Act of 1988, which officially transformed AFDC from a program to help poor women stay home with their children into a mandatory work program. Since it had taken so long to reach this point and because the changes were historic, most observers agreed that it was likely to be the last piece of welfare reform for a while. It therefore took almost everyone by surprise when, during his run for the presidency in the early 1990s, Clinton pledged to "end welfare as we know it," thus placing the issue of welfare reform at the top of his political agenda. When the Republicans took over Congress in 1994, they used the already heated attack on AFDC to support an even larger effort to dismantle the entire welfare state and redefine the role of government.

Although Parts 1 and 2 have focussed on the attacks on women and welfare, it would be a mistake to assume that women have taken these attacks lying down. Part 4 will describe their activism in some detail. However, before we turn to "the streets," we need to take a look at the universities and colleges, where feminist scholars have fought to reform the prevailing theories of the welfare state so that they might better represent the lives of women.

PART 3

THE GENDERED WELFARE STATE

In legislatures and universities across the United States, women have struggled with the issues raised by welfare reform. While welfare mothers and their advocates have agitated for less punitive and more responsive social welfare programs, feminist scholars have had to shoulder their way into debates surrounding the origins and function of the welfare state. Although women predominate among welfare clients and workers, for years the academic community remained strikingly silent on the gender issues that welfare raises. The men who dominated welfare research and policymaking approached the subject by focusing on white male workers and their female dependents. These theorists investigated workplaces, labor markets, trade unions, political parties, and other institutions that have traditionally barred women. Their research findings were generalized to women of all races, and to women and men of color.

While these analyses have made important contributions to our knowledge of the welfare state, they have focussed on the dynamics of labor markets, capitalist economics, and class struggle without paying systematic attention to the dynamics of families, to patriarchal arrangements, and to gender issues. Volumes of research document how the welfare state creates and mediates class inequality, but until feminists came on the scene we knew next to nothing about how it creates and mediates gender inequality. Social welfare may be part of the problem for women, but it could be part of the solution as well. This section reviews the feminist critiques of the liberal, social citizenship, and traditional Marxist theories of the welfare state, describes some of the feminist correctives, and then suggests social welfare policies that might better address the needs of women and men. The analysis draws on liberal, cultural (radical), and socialist feminist thinking because taken together these scholars have shown that gender matters.

GENDER MATTERS

An exploration of the long-standing but relatively unstudied relationship between women and the welfare state needs to begin with a review of four distinct but interrelated sources of gender inequality: sexism, patriarchy, the gender division of labor, and social reproduction. These key gender aspects of our social structure are important for the feminist critique presented here because they have shaped most of our societal institutions, including the welfare state. Each of the different feminist approaches emphasizes some of these dimensions more than others: the liberal feminists emphasize sexism, the cultural feminists highlight patriarchy, and the socialist feminists focus on social reproduction and the gender division of labor. However, we need to know about each of these four features of society in order to understand the relationship between women and the welfare state.

Sexism, which is central to the liberal feminist analysis of the welfare state, refers to the belief that a person's ability, intelligence, and character are rooted in biology rather than shaped by external forces; that males naturally possess more of certain desired traits and are therefore superior; and that, due to their alleged "inferiority," women can legitimately be denied equal rights and opportunities. Sexism can appear in both individual and institutional forms. Individual sexism refers to overt attitudes and behavior, from beliefs that prejudge others (i.e., prejudice) to the differential treatment of people based on their group association (i.e., discrimination). Institutional sexism refers to the ways in which laws, policies, or practices systematically create and enforce prevailing sexual inequities. Whether or not the individuals involved have sexist intentions, or are even aware of these outcomes, if institutional processes yield sexist consequences, the institution in question can be considered sexist.

Racism works in much the same way as sexism, benefiting some at the expense of others and thus perpetuating the power of a dominant group. The resulting inequality is then justified by ideologies and theories that assert that the uneven distribution of power, resources, and privileges is biologically based and therefore "natural," inevitable, and difficult to change. By dividing similarly oppressed groups that might otherwise join forces and fight for a bigger share of the proverbial pie, or even for a new and better one, both "isms" camouflage the real power of those who benefit most from keeping others down.

The concept of *patriarchy* is central to cultural feminist analysis of the welfare state.[1] While sexism underscores the unequal treatment of individuals on the basis of their sex, patriarchy speaks to the unequal distribution of power between *all* women and *all* men. Originally defined as the "rule of the father," the term has been broadened to include the structural and ideological arrangements that enable men as a group to dominate women as a group. Patriarchy is thus the institutionalization of male dominance throughout society, and as such diminishes women's control over their choices about childrearing, mothering, laboring, and loving. The distribution of the privileges of patriarchy vary sharply by class and race, so that some men benefit more than others. The strength and manifestations of patriarchal power also shift with changes in the wider social order.

Patriarchy is enforced by the ideology of gender roles. Ideology is the collection of symbols and beliefs that are integrally tied to social and political power. Ideologies are transmitted to members of a society through the language and images of everyday life, in formal institutions, and by the "isms" described above. Like all ideologies, the ideology of gender roles gives meaning to social relations, shapes how people think and act, and upholds prevailing relations of power by (among other things) rewarding conforming behavior and discrediting alternatives—such as mother-only households or lesbian couples—as wrong or even dangerous.

While remaining at the core of much feminist analysis, the concept of patriarchy has evoked considerable debate within feminist ranks. Some feminists have argued that it is difficult to operationalize and that it has embedded in it the notion of women as victims. Others have debated the roots of patriarchy, grounding it alternatively in biology, psychology, culture, social structure, and ideology. Most feminists, however, recognize that patriarchy is central to women's oppression.

The *gender division of labor* is the third source of gender inequality. It is particularly emphasized by socialist feminists, who link male domination to the economic dependence of women on men. Standard social science theories used to hold that the assignment of breadwinning roles to men and homemaking roles to women was not only natural but contributed to the smooth functioning of the family and society. Feminists generally argue that this arrangement is socially constructed—and that it is also patriarchal and oppressive to women.

The modern gender division of labor appeared in the early 1800s, as the Industrial Revolution gradually separated production for the household from production for the market. The developing factory system drew men out of the home. At the same time, family life, once intimately linked to economic activity, became a distinct and specific arena, with women in charge of parenting, homemaking, and caretaking. The shift to a market economy, and the allocation of waged work to men and domestic work to women, eventually devalued women's work in the home (as it was unwaged), and left women economically dependent on men.

A new ideology of gender roles reinforced the emerging division of labor. The social norms of the period, which I call the "family ethic,"[2] equated masculinity with waged labor, male domination, and breadwinning; and femininity with unpaid labor, female subordination, and caretaking. This arrangement was legitimized by the belief that male and female roles were biologically determined; by legal doctrines that defined women as the property of men; and by laws that barred women from the workforce, denied them the right to make contracts or own property, and excluded them from political participation, including the vote. The family ethic defined white middle- and upper-class women as fragile and pure and confined them to the home.

In the years before the Civil War, while the family ethic glorified and "protected" white middle-class women, slavery was brutalizing black women, forcing them to work in the fields and to breed children for masters who routinely tore their families apart.[3] After slavery was abolished, this double standard of womanhood continued: black women were expected to work while white middle-class women were expected to stay home.

The double standard also applied to white working-class women. Although skilled white male workers fought for a "family wage" through their unions and political parties, it was not until the end of the nineteenth century that they earned enough to be the family's sole breadwinner. In the absence of a wage that provided a man with enough income to allow his wife to stay home, raise the children, and maintain the family, many working-class women had to earn an income: young single women went to work in the new mills and factories, while wives either joined them or took in boarders, sewing, or laundry.

The family ethic persisted well into the twentieth century. When challenged by the massive entry of women into the labor force after World War II, the family ethic expanded to incorporate women's employment—but the gender roles were maintained because this work was defined as temporary, as secondary to a woman's family duties, and as an exception to the norm. In addition, women were segregated into low-paid "female" jobs and their income was labelled pin money, trousseau money, or the "second" income.

The family ethic has also survived the challenges of rising divorce rates, single motherhood, childless couples, alternative methods of conception, gay and lesbian parenting, the women's movement, and, most recently, the declining standard of living, but not without causing a backlash against women's rights. Today's call for a return to "family values" is part of an effort to restore the family ethic and its gender division of labor by stigmatizing nontraditional families and by pushing women (except welfare mothers) to return to their "rightful" place in the home.

The family ethic is the ideological glue that continues to reinforce the gender division of labor. Women are locked into traditional domestic roles and forced to remain financially, if not emotionally, dependent on men. The belief that women belong at home rationalizes the conditions that produce the economic vulnerability that keeps them there. In other words, women's presence in the home appears to "prove" that home is where women want to be and where they belong.

Social reproduction is the final source of gender inequality, and is another concept that is particularly emphasized in socialist feminist analyses of the welfare state.[4] Social reproduction refers to the way societies meet individual needs; prepare the next generation for school, work, marriage, and parenthood; and replace those who die. While many institutions play a role in social reproduction, in Western capitalist societies it is routinely expected to take place in two-parent, heterosexual homes.

The gender division of labor defines social reproduction as "women's work." Even women who work outside the home are expected to reproduce the species (procreation), to rear and socialize children so that they comply with social norms and expectations (childrearing), to purchase and prepare food, clothing, and shelter (homemaking), and to provide for family members who are too old or young to care for themselves (caretaking). In other words, women's unpaid labor in the home not only meets the family's physical and emotional needs, but it keeps the economy going by supplying a healthy, productive, and properly socialized labor force.

The concept of social reproduction became central to the socialist feminist analyses for several reasons. First, it highlighted the work women do and the relationship between women, the family, and the labor market. Second, as we will see below, it helped explain the role of the welfare state. And third, as we will see in Part 4, it showed how women's activism could develop.

FEMINIST CRITIQUES AND CORRECTIVES

The welfare state gained popularity as a subject of study in the late 1960s and 1970s, just before the social welfare system that had expanded in the postwar years began to be cut back. At first, most welfare state analyses focused on questions of labor, class, and capitalism. Scholars examined how the welfare state affected and was shaped by economic production, class divisions, and class struggle, but not how it reflected and reinforced social reproduction, the gender division of labor, and women's political struggles.

The feminist critique that was launched in the late 1970s appeared because the existing scholarship ignored these "women's issues." Resisted by male-dominated academia, feminist scholars, like the welfare mothers, had to fight back. Their critique, synthesized below, argues that traditional studies of the welfare state—covering AFDC as well as Social Security, Unemployment Insurance, and most other social programs—failed to consider (1) the roles of women, the family, and social reproduction in the origins of the welfare state; (2) the ways in which social welfare programs enforced the family ethic (as well as the work ethic); (3) the programs' differential treatment of women and men; (4) the re-creation by the welfare state of the gender and race (as well as class) hierarchies found in the wider society; and (5) the role of patriarchy in the construction of the welfare state.

The feminist critique of traditional welfare state theories was derived from the three feminist perspectives noted earlier. This review relies most heavily on the work of the socialist feminists, however, and to a lesser extent on that of the liberal feminists, because these two approaches examined the relationship between women and the welfare state in more depth than the cultural feminists. My synthesis of feminist theory, as well as the theoretical section of Part 4, represents the condensation of a very complex body of work and does not identify individual scholars (except in the notes). Such a broad overview inevitably oversimplifies many issues, pays inadequate attention to important debates among feminist thinkers, and omits many theoretical concerns. Its aim is to highlight some of the major points made and to examine some of the reasons feminist scholars felt compelled to contest the traditional views. (For those seeking a more in-depth look, the notes to this part represent a good starting place.)

BRINGING THE FAMILY IN: THE ORIGINS OF THE WELFARE STATE

The questions of how, when, and why nations create welfare states were addressed in a number of ways by scholars in the 1960s and 1970s. The three main theoretical approaches—liberal, social citizenship, and Marxist—all associated the origins of the welfare state with capitalist development. But while each understood the process somewhat differently, none paid adequate attention to the relationship between women, the family, and the state.

Liberal social science linked the development of the welfare state to the new forms of economic insecurity created by the Industrial Revolution.[5] While the emerging market economy improved the overall standard of living, it also created economic hazards that few individuals had the power to control. For one, the mechanization of industry impoverished some workers and rendered others superfluous. Families risked losing their income-earners due to old age, illness, disability, and unemployment, as well as the absence or death of a breadwinner. The forces of industrialization left wage earners dependent on the decisions of an employer, the condition of the local labor market, and the vagaries of the larger economy. Along with these new sources of economic vulnerability, the growth of crowded cities, the influx of impoverished immigrants, and rapid social change generated a myriad of social problems whose management exceeded the capacity of families, relief systems, and other existing mechanisms of support.

The mounting problems of living and working in an industrial society gradually elicited a government response. Once a nation developed an economic surplus and organizational capacity, the government gradually created new social welfare institutions to shield workers from the worst abuses of the labor market and to compensate them for such catastrophes as the loss of a job or a work-related injury. Along with private charities and voluntary organizations, the state also began to absorb more and more of the economic, educational, public health, and social service functions that had been performed by families and other local institutions. The expanding social welfare system not only helped to regulate the uncertain labor market, but also helped to stabilize the wider social order. These new programs, although never enough and often accompanied by too much social control, nevertheless improved the quality of life for many people.

The second theoretical approach to the rise of the welfare state—the social citizenship model—also holds that the move from pre-industrial to industrial society undercut traditional mechanisms of community support and created the need for new ones.[6] However, this approach argues that the need for "social integration," rather than protection against economic risk, was the prime reason for the development of the welfare state. The achievement of social integration and solidarity, however, depended on the full participation of all members of society, and this participation in turn required the acquisition of the rights of citizenship: civil rights (the right to individual liberty and equality before the law, upheld by legal institutions); political rights (the right to vote and to run for office, based in political institutions); and social rights (the right to a minimum standard of living, lodged in the welfare state). The welfare state emerged after workers struggled for civil and political rights and used these hard-won gains to demand greater economic security in the form of social rights (welfare state benefits).

Over time, the scale and scope of these rights widened and came to cover more groups: civil and political rights that were initially restricted to male landowners were extended to the working and middle class (and later to women). Similarly, social rights that were initially restricted to the poor were gradually granted to these other groups. However, the pace and extent of this expansion of social rights—that is, the growth of the welfare state—varied widely throughout Western capitalist nations, with the U.S. welfare state being one of the slowest and most meager.

Looking at the same history, traditional (pre-feminist) Marxists argued that the welfare state arose to protect capitalism from itself, rather than as an inevitable response to mounting social problems or to the enfranchisement of the masses.[7] The welfare state's development therefore reflects the interaction of three factors: industrial capitalism's need for a more efficient environment in which to operate—in particular, the need for a highly productive labor force; the struggle of the working class against exploitation; and the recognition by the propertied class that welfare programs are the price that must be paid for political stability. More specifically, the welfare state emerged to maintain the conditions necessary for profitable capital accumulation and the maintenance of social order—both of which can be jeopardized by the dynamics of capitalist production. On the one hand, capitalist profits depend heavily on the laboring capacity of workers. On the other hand, capitalists cannot be relied upon to reproduce and maintain the labor force because their profits depend on low wages, high rates of unemployment, and spending as little as possible on benefits or the work environment.

The tension between the capitalists' drive for profits and the workers' need to survive periodically threatens the productivity, if not the existence, of the workforce. When the clash between making profits and meeting human needs creates undue economic inefficiency or deep political conflict, the state often steps in, using social welfare programs to mediate the conflict. The health services, educational programs, and income-support benefits that are introduced in times of economic or political instability (as well as under other conditions) have strengthened capitalism by using the power of the state to create the conditions necessary for profitable investment, increased consumption, and social harmony.

From the perspective of the feminists who began investigating welfare in the late 1970s, the three standard explanations for the rise of the welfare state lacked a gender analysis: they minimized the importance of the family, sexist bias, and gender inequality, and failed to discuss the role that middle- and working-class women activists had played in the development of the welfare state—a subject that we will return to in Part 4.[8]

Given their interest in women, it is not surprising scholars holding all the feminist perspectives spotted the perfunctory treatment of the family in the traditional analyses of the origins of the welfare state. For instance, traditional liberal theory recognized that the government became involved in social welfare to back up families and other local systems of support that, due to the advance of industrialization, could no longer carry out all the tasks assigned to them. However, due to its preoccupation with the role of the state in protecting workers against the weaknesses of the labor market, liberal welfare state theory did not adequately situate workers in the home. Social citizenship theory's emphasis on citizenship downplayed the family in similar ways. When the family did come into the picture, it was as an afterthought, rather than as an analytic variable built into the general theory.

Traditional Marxism also gave inadequate attention to the family, and to the position of women in society in general. Reflecting its preoccupation with the production side of the equation, Marxism took women's role in the daily and inter-generational reproduction and maintenance of the working class as a given, and failed to examine the family as the site of social reproduction. Although Frederick Engels saw that women suffered as the property of men and equated women's domestic labor with "slavery," he concluded that this would change once women entered the wage labor force and after workers transformed capitalism into a socialist society.

The failure of the three traditional analyses to recognize that "families mattered" in the development of the welfare state helps explain the lack of attention to the role of social reproduction and to women's unpaid labor in the home. Socialist feminists in particular argued that the welfare state arose not only to cushion the adverse impact of industrialization (liberal theory), to foster social solidarity (social citizenship theory), and to mediate the conflict between production for profit and production for need (Marxist theory), but also to underwrite the cost of social reproduction in the home. In other words, when the imperatives of profitable production—high profits, low wages, and a degree of unemployment—came into conflict with the requirements of social reproduction, the average family's need for adequate resources to carry out its assigned caretaking and maintenance tasks forced the state to step in to shore up it up economically. In subsidizing the family and women's unpaid labor in the home, the state reinforced both the family ethic and the work ethic, and thus perpetuated the economic dependence of women on men.

Bringing families into the analysis in this way led to a reconsideration of the origins of the welfare state. Socialist feminists concluded that those standard theories that tied the rise of the welfare state to the loss of family functions were unknowingly portraying the impact of industrialization on patriarchal arrangements in the home. Prior to industrialization, the laws of marriage, property, inheritance, and public assistance placed nearly all authority in the hands of the male head of household. However, the forces of capitalist development—increased geographic mobility, smaller families, greater dependence on market wages, the employment of women, and the attachment of rights to individuals rather than family units—shattered the established bases of male domination, both inside and outside the home. While traditional analyses argued that the welfare state arose to replace the functions of the family that industrialization had undermined, socialist feminists pointed out that social welfare programs were effectively replacing *private* patriarchy, based on individual male authority in the home, with *public* patriarchy, grounded in collective control by men through the state.

GENDER BLIND: THE DIFFERENTIAL TREATMENT OF WOMEN AND MEN

The second feminist critique of the standard welfare state theories focussed on the different ways that social programs treat women and men, and the sexism this perpetuates.[9] As a result of their concerns about sex discrimination in general, liberal feminists were among the first to discover that conventional social welfare theories were gender blind: the liberal, social citizenship, and Marxist discussions of social welfare, like social policy itself, all presumed a male standard based on waged work as the norm for all welfare state recipients, and then generalized their findings to all women (and men of color)—as if race and gender differences did not exist. Because of this, and despite their different foci, each of the traditional theories presented an inaccurate picture of women's relationships to the welfare state.

One male bias found in both liberal and social citizenship theory stemmed from the twin premises that (1) waged work is the prime way to contribute to society and (2) social welfare policy exists to protect workers and their families from the risk of lost income or to compensate those who have contributed to society but are without financial support through no fault of their own. The presumption was that welfare state participants were male breadwinners and that women were dependents of men; at the same time, the ways in which the gender division of labor keeps women from qualifying for the more substantial welfare state benefits were obscured.

Although the standard theories looked at the relationship between the welfare state and the labor market, they all failed to recognize that wage and employment structures were gendered

Food and clothing being distributed at the Surplus Commodities Distribution Center in Springfield, Massachusetts, 1938. Note the sign on the left which indicates that even in the WPA, the traditional two-parent family ethic was upheld vigorously. [National Archives]

in ways that penalized female recipients. For example, liberal feminists pointed out that because Social Security and Unemployment Insurance benefits are wage-based, women receive lower benefits than men. By not compensating for the male/female wage gap, which is the result of sex discrimination in the labor market, the welfare state reproduces it. Second, feminists showed that it is harder for women to receive full benefits because of the ways in which the programs are employment-driven. Given their caretaking duties, women have a harder time than most men accumulating the ten years of work experience needed to qualify for Social Security retirement benefits. Similarly, Unemployment Insurance does not cover most of the part-time, temporary, or intermittent jobs that many women "choose" in order to care for their families. Nor does it cover the husband or wife who leaves his or her job to follow a spouse to a new city—a pattern much more common among women than men. Finally, the discussion of the risks of the labor market found in these theories presumes that most workers are men: pregnancy, childrearing, and caretaking responsibilities are rarely considered. These risks, like sexual harassment and sex-segregated jobs, are faced primarily by women. Women need protection from these and other failures of the labor market. They also need protection from failures of marriage (such as divorce, desertion, lack of child support from a noncustodial parent, and violence in the home), all of which may impoverish women and leave them to raise children on their own.

The social citizenship analysis of the social welfare system also failed to consider the male biases in its definition of citizenship.[10] More specifically, the theory accepted past and present measures of social citizenship—the capacity to bear arms, to own property, or to work in paid employment—that exclude women. Moreover, it uncritically defined the self-supporting white male wage-earner as the "ideal citizen" and argued that an individual's rights, identity, and social status are established by ties to the labor market. Rarely did the theory consider that these rules of citizenship exclude economically dependent individuals, including both women whose independence has been circumscribed by their economic dependence on men and African-American men and women whose independence has been circumscribed by racism. Nor did it consider other important sources of rights, identity, and status, such as a person's role in the family and community.

The social citizenship theory privileges (white) men in still another way by arguing that the development of the welfare state (or social rights) depended on the working class's prior acquisition—through political struggle—of civil and political rights. This understanding of history ignores the fact that women, people of color, and other politically disenfranchised groups have had less and subordinated access to civil and political rights. Nor does it explain how women in the United States played a major role in the development of the welfare state *before* they won the vote in 1919.

Feminists pointed out that the (male) concept of citizenship places women in a double bind. Women have to demand the social rights of citizenship on the grounds of equality (i.e., on equal terms with men) or on the grounds of difference (i.e., based on their different talents, needs, and responsibilities "as women"). In the first instance they end up as "lesser men," because in patriarchal societies women lack equal opportunity to compete for jobs, income, prestige, and power. In the second instance they risk less than full recognition, because patriarchal society devalues women's identity, status, and contributions.

The male bias in traditional Marxist theory stemmed from the priority it gave to class over patriarchal power. The early Marxists, who predated the modern welfare state in Europe and the United States, argued that women became oppressed when capitalism turned them into male property.[11] They argued that the exploitation of women and men derived from the same source, and assumed that their oppression could be understood in the same terms. Thus the entry of women into the workforce would lead to their emancipation not simply by reducing their economic dependence on men, but by engaging them in the struggle to transform capitalism and eliminate the private property on which their subordination was based.

The contemporary Marxists who studied the modern welfare state carried this gender-blind analysis forward.[12] They analyzed who benefits and who loses from the class organization of the social welfare system, but they seldom asked who benefits and who loses from the ways in which society organizes the reproduction of the labor force, the consumption of goods and services, and the rearing of the children—that is, who benefits and who loses from the division of labor by gender. Failing to acknowledge the power of patriarchy *independent* of capitalism, they rarely took up issues of women's oppression, gender differences, or the gendered features of the welfare state.

TWIN DYNAMICS: THE WORK ETHIC
AND THE FAMILY ETHIC

The third feminist critique of traditional welfare state theories targeted their singular preoccupation with the work ethic. Traditional approaches not only assumed that all workers were men, but also devoted a great deal of their analysis to the relationship between welfare state benefits and market wages. Liberal theorists argued that welfare state benefits were below the lowest prevailing wage so that no one would choose public assistance or social insurance benefits over low-paid work. Social citizenship analysts added that, in varying degrees, Western industrial nations kept benefits down in order to reduce the leverage of workers vis-à-vis capital and to weaken their capacity to bargain for higher wages. Marxists argued that meager social welfare benefits increased the size of the labor pool, held wages down, kept workers in line, and otherwise enabled capital to exploit labor.

Parts 1 and 2 have already described some of the ways in which public assistance programs reinforced the work ethic by keeping women off AFDC and thus tied to the labor market. Other social welfare programs, such as Social Security and Unemployment Insurance, also reinforce the work ethic by favoring those who have worked or who are considered without work through no fault of their own (such as the young, old, sick, and disabled), while penalizing those deemed able but unwilling to work. But it took feminist theory to show that social welfare programs enforce the family ethic as well.[13] Nearly all feminists agree that in the United States, as in most Western industrial countries, the structure of welfare benefits keeps women economically tied to marriage and the family, and reinforces traditional gender roles. Both liberal and socialist feminists have shown that social welfare programs—including AFDC, Social Security, and Unemployment Insurance—favor the heterosexual, two-parent family by treating women recipients differently based on their marital status. Thus women who form and sustain traditional households are rewarded and those who depart from prescribed roles are punished. Just as welfare programs ensure that working people do better than those on welfare, so households headed by married or previously married women, such as widows, fare better than households headed by single mothers, abandoned women, or divorced wives, all of whom are considered able but unwilling to marry, and, often, responsible for a family's break up.

Feminists have focussed on the family ethic not only because it adds to women's oppression by enforcing their economic dependence on men, but because it inaccurately assumes that the family is a stable unit whose members pool and distribute their income and power equally.[14] This belief that the family is harmonious and equitable is demonstrably false—one need only look at the nation's high rates of divorce and separation, at the widespread violence against women and children, and at the frequent disputes over rights and responsibilities in the home. To feminists, conflicts within the family are a manifestation of patriarchal power in the same way that conflicts between workers and employers are expressions of the power relations of class.

Feminists of color put forward a slightly different analysis. They pointed out that when it comes to African-American women, the welfare state enforces the work ethic, but *violates* the family ethic.[15] As we saw in Parts 1 and 2, social welfare policies either excluded African-American women or forced them to work for low wages, even as it encouraged white middle-class women to stay at home. This double standard not only channeled black women into exploitative jobs, but kept them from living according to the rules of the family ethic, if they so desired, by staying home. In other words, welfare state policies, combined with racial discrimination, effectively denied black women the opportunity to choose, as many white women did, to trade the constraints of economic dependence on men for the protections that family life offered to women. This insight was especially important because it showed how the forces of domination work differently in black and white communities: among blacks, the family often functions as a refuge from a racist society and its role as a site of resistance to racial oppression may therefore override the oppression of women that it may also entail.

RECREATING GENDER AND RACE HIERARCHIES

The fourth feminist critique of the standard welfare state theories focused on the question of domination rather than discrimination—that is, on the way the welfare state recreates gender, race, and class hierarchies rather than its differential treatment of women and men. The standard welfare-state theories all examined power, but only as it pertained to class relations. They thus accepted the two-tiered structure of the welfare state described in Part 1—universal social insurance for the middle class and means-tested public assistance for the poor—as reflecting wider class inequalities. But the liberal and social citizenship theories argued that the protection against the risks of the market economy provided by the welfare state soften these class differences by cushioning poverty and promoting social integration. In contrast, Marxists argued that the welfare state does little to change the unequal distribution of income and wealth, and that because its programs often quiet social unrest, it enforces the power of the ruling class.

Feminists, on the other hand, argued that class is not the only fault line in the welfare state.[16] As we have seen, the welfare state incorporates the family ethic (which supports the economic dependence of women on men), subsidizes social reproduction in the home (based on the division of labor by gender), and rewards men's paid labor in the market over women's unpaid labor in the home. The welfare state therefore actively reinforces the social and economic bases of male domination and female subordination. Since the employment-based distribution of benefits inevitably recreates the inequalities of the labor market, the welfare state reinforces the unequal power relations based on the differential treatment of workers based on gender.

The two-tiered structure of the welfare state also reproduces the inequalities of race found in wider society because the more disadvantaged members of society—those who are more likely to be deprived of an adequate income by racial discrimination—are relegated to the stigmatized and locally administered public assistance programs. Since these programs serve those who have not been able to work during their prime years due to illness, disability, lack of marketable skills, or childrearing responsibilities, the poor, women, and people of color are overrepresented on their rolls. Further, to the extent that both employment and social welfare benefits are based on a person's citizenship status, this extends to immigrants, including the growing number of foreign-born persons of color.

WHAT ABOUT PATRIARCHY AND GENDER OPPRESSION?

The preceding feminist critiques targeted a mix of liberal and socialist feminist concerns about the lack of attention to women and the family in the scholarship on the welfare state, its unfair treatment of women relative to men, its support for traditional two-parent families and stereotypical gender roles, and its ability to reproduce the hierarchies of gender and race as well as class. The final critique shifts the focus from the impact of the welfare state on the lives of women to the relationship between the welfare state and the dynamics of capitalism and patriarchy. This critique, which came from the socialist feminists, went through several stages, or what I will call here conversations. The first defined the welfare state as an institution that oppressed and subordinated women by reinforcing patriarchal controls. The second argued that the welfare state mediates conflicts between capitalism and patriarchy. Building on the insights of both, the third added that the welfare state has the potential to emancipate as well as to control women. It is useful to review these conversations not only because they show the development of the feminist analysis of the welfare state, but because the last conversation sets the stage for moving on from our analysis of the struggle of feminists in the academy to the struggle of women in the streets.

Conversation 1: Reinforcing Patriarchy. Feminist theorists uncovered the patriarchal underpinnings of the welfare state early on and showed how its policies fostered the oppression of women.[17] They developed their theory about the role of patriarchy by studying the social welfare system itself. One of their first insights was that social policy typically defines women in terms of their biological functions, and uses state power to "protect" women as reproducers of the species and socializers of the next generation. For example, during the Progressive Era many states passed labor laws to protect women on the grounds that poor working conditions jeopardized their capacity to bear and rear children. Despite repeated efforts, social reformers failed to get these laws—which shortened the work day, limited night shifts, restricted the number of pounds a worker could lift, and mandated that employers provide seats—extended to men, who also needed protection from unsafe jobs. Two other programs that were enacted at the same time as the protective labor laws—the Mothers' Pensions discussed in Part 2 and the Sheppard Towner Maternal and Child Health Act of 1921 (an early federal public health nursing program for mothers and children)—also defined women as childbearers and childrearers who needed "protection" from the labor market.

These early efforts did little to alleviate gender oppression. Many employers used the protective labor laws as an excuse not to hire women, to pay them lower wages, or to send them back home. As we saw in Part 1, Mothers' Pensions evolved into ADC, and, as a program for single women only, was highly vulnerable to attack; the Sheppard Towner program lasted only a few years before Congress closed it down.

The Social Security Act of 1935 perpetuated the biological construction of womanhood by serving most women as mothers and wives, and by assisting them primarily when they were caring for children or spouses. For example, for many years the AFDC program did not aid a pregnant woman until her child was born. Similarly, Medicaid did not cover pregnant women until Congress added maternity benefits in 1980. To this day, a single woman on AFDC and a surviving spouse under age sixty-five on Social Security lose benefits when their youngest children reach the age of eighteen. This "widow's gap" leaves adult women who do not have spouses or children without any governmental income support unless they qualify for benefits as disabled or become eligible for local home relief.

The conversation about reinforcing patriarchy also showed how welfare state programs shore up patriarchal controls by perpetuating the economic dependence of women on men.[18] Until 1970, when the women's movement forced the courts to override the policy on the grounds of discrimination, Social Security rules made it difficult for a working woman to claim Social Security benefits for a dependent *male* spouse: it had to be proven that the husband's earnings had supplied less than one-fourth of the couple's income during the year prior to the wife's retirement (or death). Yet the wives of employed men were not required to undergo this "support test." Further, some of the Social Security Act programs do more than presume the economic dependence of women on men—they actively reward it. First, as noted earlier, social welfare programs promote women's economic dependence by penalizing those who challenge the family ethic. The retirement benefits favor one- earner over two-earner couples and lifetime homemakers over working wives. Many women receive a larger benefit as dependent spouses (one-half their husbands' grants) than they can qualify for on the basis of their own work records. As late as 1985, more than one-third of the women who were eligible for benefits based on their own records received them instead as wives or widows of workers because of their lower wages. Working women who have paid into the Social Security system for years complain they gain nothing in retirement that they could not receive "for free" on the basis of their husbands' earnings and that they are no better off than homemakers who have paid no Social Security taxes at all. This would be different if benefits were available to women in their own right, rather than as dependents living in male-headed family units.

Conversation 2: Mediating Conflict. As the second conversation about patriarchy and capitalism commenced, the discussion

Applying for welfare, New York City, 1985. [George Cohen/Impact Visuals]

became more complex. Instead of arguing that the welfare state simply reinforced patriarchal rule, feminists began to see patriarchy and capitalism as two independent systems that could work in concert *or as rivals*, and that conflicts between them were often mediated by the welfare state.[19]

When the forces of patriarchy and capitalism work in concert, the gender division of labor is enforced, to the advantage of both systems. Take women's labor: women's unpaid work in the home benefits individual men by relieving them of the responsibility for raising children, managing the family's consumption, and maintaining the family in other noneconomic ways. These services are not part of men's gender-assigned roles, and men with resources can even buy them. Wives also meet the personal, sexual, and emotional needs of men, and their commitment to the home keeps them from competing with men for better paying jobs and jobs with more responsibility. The state upholds the home as a refuge for men, but for women it can often mean economic dependence, the double day, or domestic violence.

While "serving" patriarchy, this gendered family arrangement also "serves" capitalism. For one, women at home become a flexible pool of workers who can be pulled in and out of the labor force as needed—to fill labor shortages, to compete with male workers, and to otherwise lower labor costs by pushing, or keeping, wages down. Women's unpaid labor in the home also ensures the maintenance of the current and future labor force. Finally, employers use the fact that women have family responsibilities to justify hiring them in low-paid, sex-segregated jobs, which once again benefits capitalism by keeping wages down and benefits patriarchy by keeping women economically insecure. As we have seen, when families cannot survive on what they earn, welfare can shore them up so that they will continue to carry out the social and reproductive tasks on which both systems depend.

In the tug of war over women's labor, the two systems also create many conflicts within and between themselves. For example, as industrial capitalism advanced, its demand for low-paid workers drew more and more women out of the home. Once women became permanent members of the workforce, they were no longer the reserve army that could be brought into the labor market at will to drive wages down. Having achieved a critical mass, working women joined unions and otherwise mobilized against the inequality of opportunity and rights on the job and in wider society.[20] In addition to both serving *and* challenging capitalist control, the employment of women weakened patriarchal controls in the home. Working wives deprived individual men of women's domestic services and increased women's economic autonomy.

Instead of simply "servicing" capitalism or patriarchy separately, feminists concluded the welfare state helps to *mediate* the competing demands for women's home and market labor. One way it does this is by categorizing women as "deserving" and "undeserving" of aid based on their marital status. We have seen how some social welfare programs (like AFDC) send poor and working-class women into the workforce, while others (like Old Age Insurance) encourage middle-class wives and mothers to stay home. This suggests that the welfare state tries to reconcile the imperatives of both systems so that each is served, at least in part. These mediation efforts fall especially hard on African-American women, who are more likely than white women to end up with low and stigmatized benefits.

The welfare state mediates the conflicting demands of capitalism and patriarchy as well when women become organized and force the government to address their need for labor laws, equal pay, a minimum wage, childcare, family leave, educational rights, and greater control over their bodies. That many of these demands remain only partially fulfilled, and are now threatened across the board, suggests the extent of the resistance to women challenging domination at home and exploitation on the job.

Conversation 3: Emancipating Women. The third conversation about the welfare state moved from defining it as instrument of mediation to seeing it as arena of political struggle. Once it became clear that some welfare state policies could weaken the power of patriarchy and capitalism, feminists realized that welfare was an institution that *both* regulated the lives of women *and* created the conditions for their emancipation. Drawing on studies by the social citizenship school, which showed the differential effect of meager and generous welfare systems on the power of their recipients, these feminists concluded that the welfare state can serve the interests of dominant *and* subordinate groups at different times and in different ways, and that welfare programs can therefore have both regulatory and emancipatory possibilities.[21]

The social citizenship theorists maintain that access to social welfare benefits is an important source of power because it enables workers to subsist without having to rely fully on the market, and that this reduced vulnerability to employers has the potential to increase workers' power vis-à-vis capital and even to alter class relations. Feminists recognize this dynamic but point out that it operates differently for those who need to gain full access into the market in the first place. This not only means equal opportunity but equal pay for comparable work, equal voice in the workplace, and the caretaking supports needed to balance work and family responsibilities. Having once become full-fledged players in the market, women can then use welfare state benefits to enhance their political leverage, helping them to negotiate for decision-making power in the workplace.

But even this will not be enough as women still have to negotiate for power in the home as well. Just as cash benefits can increase a worker's leverage in the market, so they can increase a woman's leverage at home and thereby lessen the hold of patriarchy as well as capitalism. By reducing women's financial vulnerability, the welfare state can free women to bargain, individually and collectively, with men, and to enter and leave relationships on their own terms. Even more critically, public programs can contribute to women's emancipation by enabling them to maintain independent households thereby allowing them true autonomy. If the welfare state were to develop in these ways, it could free women from economic dependence on men *and* markets, embolden them to take risks at home *and* on the job, and alter gender as well as class relations.

This proposal remains controversial even among feminists, however. Some argue that women who accept welfare benefits exchange dependence on men for dependence on the state—and remain poor because welfare benefits are so low. Others argue that while dependence on men isolates women, dependence on the state brings them together, both as clients and as employees.[22] Their shared poverty and status as recipients can create the basis for collective action among welfare recipients and workers—if not together, then independently. In Part 4, we will examine the activism of poor, working, and middle-class women—both white women and women of color—to show how they first turned the basic need for food, clothing, and shelter, and then the welfare state itself, into an arena of political struggle.

PART 4

FIGHTING BACK: FROM THE LEGISLATURE TO THE ACADEMY TO THE STREETS

When you hear the word organizer, leader, rebel, or participant, what type of person comes to mind? These words typically evoke images of white men because for centuries most people believed that women did not, and should not, fill these activist roles.[1] It was not that women were not activists, however, but that their activism was hidden. The traditional, liberal, social citizenship, and Marxist theories all addressed social conflict and, despite their different interpretations, they consistently located political struggle within established organizations, movements, and institutions, all of which excluded women. Having failed to look for, much less locate, women's activism where it in fact took place, they found few women activists; they then decided that this must mean that women are conservative, politically unmotivated, and thus unworthy of study. This exclusion of women from the traditional scholarship on activism not only distorts the historical record, but disempowers women by denying them knowledge of an important part of their heritage.

The liberal political theorists dealt with the role of social conflict by minimizing it. They argued that industrialization eliminated the most basic sources of tension between workers and employers, and generated the political mechanisms needed to resolve the new conflicts that emerged.[2] It was not that discord disappeared, but that technology narrowed the economic gap between the haves and have-nots, and generated a set of political institutions and a shared body of ideas, beliefs, and values that effectively replaced class conflict. The welfare state emerged naturally from a process of mediating conflict, the result of agreement among diverse social groups that social welfare provision was necessary to protect and compensate individuals and families for the risks they incurred while living and working in a market economy.

The social citizenship theorists agreed that welfare state benefits were won politically. Less interested than their liberal counterparts in showing that democratic societies have no need for class conflict and more willing to acknowledge the role of "pressure from below," they suggested that political conflict was in fact critical to the development of the welfare state.[3] As we saw in Part 3, their analysis held that social rights (e.g., social welfare programs) emerged from political struggles that were in turn predicated on earlier successful battles for legal and political rights. Having fought for and won these democratic rights of citizenship, male workers insisted on economic security, which included a government-protected, minimal standard of living. Governments responded to the pressure by smoothing out the rough edges of capitalism and ensuring that market inequality did not undermine economic stability, political harmony, and social solidarity. To the extent that these hard-won social welfare benefits had the potential to insulate workers against market forces and provide them with leverage in their struggles with employers, they became a power resource that could embolden workers individually and collectively to take the risks involved in fighting economic exploitation.

The traditional Marxist theorists focused more directly on conflict as *class* struggle, which they argued arose from the contradictions of capitalism. One of these contradictions—the contradiction between the private nature of profitable production and the "social" character of work—made collective action possible.[4] This is because the continued accumulation of capital moved economic production to ever larger factories, thereby bringing workers together in one place and exposing them to their shared exploitation and a common enemy. A second contradiction—that between production for profit and production for need—also created the potential for collective action. As we saw in Part 2, profitable capital accumulation requires certain levels of unemployment to keep profits up and labor costs down. Because this leads to an unequal distribution of income and wealth and deprives workers of an adequate standard of living, it periodically stimulates demands for higher wages, government regulation of the market, and greater access to political power. To forestall such turmoil, business and government may try to repress striking workers and popular movements, or they may try to diffuse the unrest by meeting at least some of the workers' needs. The resulting reforms become the building blocks of the welfare state. But the outcome of this struggle is neither inevitable nor predetermined; it is the result of a contest between the demands of capital and those of popular movements, as mediated by the state.

THE FEMINIST CORRECTIVE

The discussion of social conflict in all three traditional theories focused on established political institutions—primarily trade unions, electoral parties, social movements, and the state—and therefore missed the activism of women, which often took place in other arenas. It was only when feminists began to investigate the "spaces" that women inhabit—their clubs, auxiliaries, workplaces, unions, and social networks—that they discovered a long and inspiring history of activism. White middle-class women's activism surfaced first because most scholars expected these women to be the most important and because privileged women left behind the kinds of materials—letters, diaries, and organizational files—that historians depend on to piece the past together. Gradually, however, feminists began to capture the collective activism of working women,[5] community-based homemakers,[6] and welfare state clients,[7] as well as that of the middle-class reformers who worked in women's organizations and large-scale women's movements.

As they uncovered women's activism, feminist scholars began to see how the gender division of labor structures the activism of men and women differently. Although both men and women become active when the contradictions between economic production and social reproduction (described in Part 3) prevent them from carrying out their gendered obligations, the locus of their activism is different. The standard male-oriented theories presumed that all political struggle takes place at the point of production and therefore focused on workplace issues. Workers typically took action through their unions—for instance, when low wages and unsafe working conditions prevented them from performing their breadwinning responsibilities. But feminists found that women also engaged in struggle at the point of consumption.[8] Women, especially working-class women, became active when they were not able to secure the food, clothing, shelter, or other resources they needed to carry out their homemaking and caretaking responsibilities. To carry out their socially assigned tasks, women engaged in collective protest at local grocery stores, housing agencies, and welfare offices. Because this activism was often sporadic, sometimes spontaneous, not always highly organized, and rarely sustained, many scholars and political pundits had dismissed it as politically insignificant. However, as the French historian George Rudé reminds us, under certain conditions small everyday collective actions can have far-reaching effects and can create unanticipated possibilities for social change.[9]

The following account of middle- and working-class women's activism "at the point of consumption" is far from complete. Nevertheless, it will provide us with an important glimpse of the collective actions taken by women of different classes and races, and the relationship between their concerns and the expanding welfare state. Even before the advent of substantial government aid, women were active when their families needed food, clothing, and shelter, or economic and racial justice. As the state increasingly underwrote the costs of social reproduction in the home, women began to target the welfare state. The gender division of labor, the tasks of social reproduction, and in some cases the shared status of being "on welfare" encouraged women to unite to enforce their rights. Thus women turned both their communities and the welfare state into arenas of political struggle.

MIDDLE-CLASS WOMEN TAKE ACTION

The gender division of labor that sent men into the labor market and isolated women in their homes led directly to the exclusion of women from the male sphere of formal politics. The social networks and female "culture" that then developed among women were highly supportive of social activism and social reform.[10] In the years before the Civil War, women could not vote or join political parties, but religious and "moral reform" activities were considered suitable. Evangelist revivals swept the nation beginning in the 1820s, becoming one of the earliest "movements" to draw women out of the home. Although the revivals were led by men, women filled the churches, published the religious tracts, and founded the Sunday schools. Women also created roles for themselves in the moral reform movement that evangelism encouraged. For example, driven by notions of female moral superiority, the New England American Female Moral Reform Society (which claimed 445 auxiliaries) and other such organizations worked to rehabilitate prostitutes and eliminate sin. Women also played leading roles in the abolition and temperance movements, as well as in organizations that assisted the poor and mentally ill.

After the Civil War, white middle-class women became active in charity associations, government boards, and the suffrage movement. From 1870 to 1900, they joined the National Women's Suffrage Association and the more conservative American Women Suffrage Association, and conducted 480 campaigns in thirty-three states. The Women's Christian Temperance Union (WCTU) drew even more women into the militant fight against alcohol and saloons, arguing that male drinking depleted household funds. By 1900, the WCTU had over 168,000 dues-paying members in 7,000 locals in forty-eight states.

In addition, scores of women attended the art and literature discussions organized by the women's clubs that proliferated beginning in the late 1860s.[11] By the 1890s, these clubs had coalesced into a national organization, the General Federation of Women's Clubs (GFWC). By 1911, GFWC-affiliated clubs had involved women in cultural, civic, and social welfare activities in towns and cities in all forty-eight states. Women also founded the National Consumers' League (1890s), the Congress of Mothers (1897), the Women's Trade Union League (1903), new suffrage organizations, neighborhood settlement houses, and many other social welfare and civic organizations.

With its ties to the grassroots, this network of women and organizations suggested the direction that activism would take among white middle-class women. Barred from careers in academia, business, and the professions, many educated women carved out an area of expertise as social reformers.[12] By the early 1900s, these women had expanded their arena of responsibility from the home to the larger community. Some groups, led by the National American Women's Suffrage Association (NAWSA) and the National Women's Party (NWP), believed that women should be treated as equals with men and therefore focused nearly exclusively on women's rights, especially the vote (finally won in 1919). Other groups believed that working women and mothers of young children needed special protection because they differed from men,[13] and led small and large battles against slums, dirty milk, and child labor, and for clean cities, decent housing, health insurance, shorter work days, and the minimum wage. These women justified their own activism with the argument that their socialization left them better equipped than men to look out for the welfare of humanity and especially suited for "municipal housekeeping"—a word they often used for social reform. Referred to today as "maternalists," members of this network staffed the settlement houses, supported trade unions, and engaged in a wide range of research, lobbying, and community work. Some, such as Julia Lathrop, the first director of the Children's Bureau, moved into important public posts. Many of these white women and their spiritual descendants carried the reform tradition forward when they worked for Franklin Roosevelt and the New Deal in the 1930s.

African-American women were also active reformers.[14] If gender segregation fostered female social reform organizations among white women, racial segregation forced African Americans to form their own networks. The mobilization of black women had deep roots in the church and drew on the tradition of slave women's networks, free black women's associations, and anti-slavery work. Driven by "duty" and "obligation to the race," black women organized on behalf of what they referred to as "racial uplift," i.e., charity, self-improvement through social service, education, and progress. Before the Civil War, black church women raised funds, organized voluntary missionary societies, and taught Sunday school. Free African-American women also participated in black-led anti-slavery, suffrage, and temperance organizations, and occasionally those organized by whites, although they frequently encountered hostility and outright exclusion. After the Civil War, middle-class African-American women worked to bring resources to the thousands of emancipated but impoverished former slaves, most of whom lived in the rural South. Almost every black women's organization worked to alleviate one or more of the many social problems afflicting an increasingly urban, impoverished, politically powerless, and segregated black population.

By the turn of the century, black people were suffering rampant racial repression: lynching, white primaries, race riots, and urban poverty. In response to the deteriorating condition of "the race," black women established at least as many voluntary associations as their white counterparts, and possibly even more, although they lacked similar resources or political connections. Nonetheless, this network of women's clubs, church organizations, and mutual-aid societies provided the foundation for powerful national organizations, including the National Association of Colored Women (NACW), founded in 1896. By 1914, the NACW represented 50,000 middle-class, educated black women in twenty-eight federations and over 1,000 clubs. The NACW platform ranged from anti-lynching campaigns to refuting negative stereotypes of black women as sexually loose to fighting for women's suffrage and other social reforms. Its members helped their communities establish separate educational and healthcare facilities, settlement houses, and social service organizations. The women in the NACW were also instrumental in the formation of the National Association of Colored People (NAACP) in 1910 and the National Urban League in 1911. Others joined the women's arm of the more separatist Universal Negro Improvement Association (UNIA), headed by Amy Jacques Garvey, Marcus Garvey's wife. Like their white counterparts, black women later worked in the New Deal—for instance, the National Council of Negro Women, formed by Mary McLeod Bethune in 1935, became the most important black women's lobby in Washington, D.C., and Roosevelt appointed Bethune head of the Office of Minority Affairs in the National Youth Administration at a time when few blacks of either gender held high political office.

There was a potential for cooperation between the white and black women's networks because both espoused maternalist values, endorsed a strict work ethic, and promoted services for the poor. But these shared values could not overcome the racial divide. While white women's organizations ignored the issue of race, it was *the* central issue for the African-American women reformers, who believed that race, poverty, and gender were inextricably intertwined. The black women espoused a maternalism that to a certain extent mirrored that of whites, but they were more accepting of single motherhood and of women having to work outside the home, and therefore opposed making income tests or moralistic behavioral standards prerequisites for government help. They upheld the family ethic not as a behavioral prescription, but because it was a means by which women could claim respect and justice in white America.

Black women's groups occasionally made overtures to white women's organizations, only to be ignored or slighted. For instance, when the white women's organizations prepared an exhibit for the Colombian Exposition at the 1893 Chicago World's Fair, they turned down a request from the black women's clubs to be represented on the board. The next year, the General Federation of Women's Clubs refused to let a well-known black woman—who was representing an established black women's group from Boston—into their convention. Some white suffragists pandered to southern segregationists, arguing that the votes of native-born, educated white women could be used to outweigh those of uneducated blacks in the South and immigrants in the North. Others supported the use of literacy or educational qualifications to reduce the number of such voters. A controversy arose over the participation of black women in a suffrage parade in 1913, and in the early 1920s a major suffrage organization, the National Women's Party, excluded blacks. Even those white women who privately deplored discrimination tacitly accepted the exclusion of African-Americans, and African-American women reformers came to regard their white counterparts with considerable distrust.

What impact did these women, white and black, have on the welfare state? Feminist scholars have answered this question differently. Some have suggested that they institutionalized government intervention on behalf of women and children and therefore helped pave the way for a broader welfare state.[15] Others contend that, although well-intentioned, they left a harmful legacy: for instance, Mothers' Pensions stigmatized single mothers, while employers used protective labor laws to exclude women from better paying jobs.[16] Still others argue that by alleviating the worst miseries of the poor, the reformers stood in the path of more militant demands.[17] In terms of the maternalist strategy itself, some scholars have argued that it idealized motherhood and reinforced women's traditional roles, while others maintain that the women reformers knowingly extolled the virtues of private domesticity in order to legitimize their own activism, which violated prevailing gender norms, and disarm resistance to their proposals, which called for a greater role for the state.[18] Regardless of the reformers' intent, however, it is generally agreed that they helped create highly gendered notions of women's citizenship on the one hand, and deepened the state's involvement in the private lives of less privileged women on the other.

POOR AND WORKING-CLASS WOMEN RISE UP ANGRY

Working-class women had their own social welfare agenda in the late nineteenth and early twentieth centuries, one that arose directly from the conditions of *their* lives. For instance, many employed women joined unions and demanded better wages and working conditions. In 1909, in one of the more dramatic actions, 20,000 New York City shirtwaist-makers, almost all women (many young and immigrant), staged a militant thirteen-week strike. The "uprising of 20,000," as it became known, forced employers to deal with the newly formed International Ladies' Garment Workers' Union.

In the early twentieth century, as younger single women were becoming militant on the job, mothers and wives—mostly but not entirely immigrants—engaged in collective action in their communities when economic conditions prevented them from carrying out their family responsibilities.[19] For example, they organized food boycotts and rent strikes that were aimed at local merchants and landlords.[20] One of the earliest, the 1902 food boycott, lasted for almost a month. Inside of one day, thousands of women streamed through the streets of New York's Lower East Side, breaking into kosher butcher shops, flinging meat into the streets, and refusing to buy their goods until the prices came down. The protest quickly spread to neighborhoods in Brooklyn and the Bronx. To keep the boycott going, the women called mass meetings, canvassed their neighborhoods, set up picket lines, and raised funds. When, during the protests, 20,000 people gathered for a demonstration, the *New York Times* called for speedy police action against this "dangerous class"—the women, according to the *Times*, "were very ignorant" and "mostly speak a foreign language." The police arrested seventy women and fifteen men.

The 1902 meat boycott was not an isolated event but the forerunner of many other price-driven protests. In 1904, 1907, and 1908, housewives organized rent strikes in New York, Philadelphia, Boston, and Providence, Rhode Island. In 1910, Jewish women in Providence declared war on the kosher butchers, and in August 1914 over 1,000 Italians in Providence took to the streets and brought pasta prices down after shattering a wholesaler's shop windows and throwing his stock of macaroni into the street. World War I price increases sparked militant neighborhood boycotts and mass demonstrations by women in Boston, Chicago, Philadelphia, and many other cities. The high cost of living drew local women into the Mother's Anti-High Price League, organized by the Socialist Party, which among other things demanded a government response—in this case food assistance. The NACW and NAACP helped lead similar protests in black communities.[21]

The women who took part in these boycotts and strikes turned their status as housewives and their neighborhood networks to good advantage. Although the housewives were not necessarily sympathetic to either trade unions or left politics, they nevertheless felt compelled to take action against the high prices that had eroded their buying power, forced them to work outside the home, and otherwise interfered with their ability to perform their domestic responsibilities. The communities accepted, and even expected, these militant actions because the merchants and landlords were members of the same ethnic groups and as such were expected not to take advantage of their customers. In other words, the assumptions of a "moral economy" in which mutual obligations governed consumption effectively legitimized the boycotts.

The "consumer economy" that replaced this "moral economy" after World War I created a new set of social expectations for women. Electrification, refrigeration, indoor plumbing, and the telephone transformed housework. To sell new goods and services to a public still wedded to habits of thrift, or too poor to buy much, business and industry built supermarkets, began to extend credit, and advertised.[22] Advertisers portrayed the American standard of living as the model for all families, and targeted women because they were the family shoppers. A "feminine mystique" was created, one that defined housework as an expression of a woman's personality and love of her family, and that linked identity, status, and fulfillment to material acquisition. Convinced by Madison Avenue of the benefits of consumption, women of all classes began to demand more goods and services for their families.[23]

The cost-of-living protests that resumed immediately after the end of World War I were thus driven less by retribution for merchants who had violated the rules of the moral economy than by the discrepancy between the promises of consumerism and the realities of rising prices. The wives of the more skilled and therefore better paid workers were especially frustrated, and some turned to the trade union's women's auxiliaries for help. These auxiliaries, which had begun to support male workers, became a way for women to become involved in the central political, economic, and social questions of the day.

One of the more visible women's auxiliaries was organized in the 1920s by the wives of railroad workers who belonged to the Machinist Union. With chapters in thirty-five states, the District of Columbia, and several Canadian provinces, the machinist's wives demanded a "saving wage," rather than a "living wage," so that they could take advantage of buying on credit to purchase appliances and other products that would enhance their families' standard of living. The wives of the men in the Brotherhood of Sleeping Car Porters, the only black-led union in the country at the time, also wanted to participate in the new consumer culture. The Sleeping Car Porters' auxiliary, which was known as the Women's Economic Council, also assisted families having problems with employers, formed alliances with elite black women, and addressed the black community's concerns about race.

By the mid-1920s, all the more socially conscious women's auxiliaries had begun to call for government-sponsored maternal and healthcare programs for children, for local health departments, and for children's bureaus. In 1928, there were enough active groups for the National Women's Trade Union League (NWTUL), an alliance of working women and middle-class reformers linked to the labor movement, to call the first national conference of trade union auxiliaries.[24]

But the major protest against rising prices and unfulfilled dreams took place in tenant and consumer organizations. These, like the auxiliaries, increasingly targeted the welfare state.[25] Large numbers of women were recruited from the Community Councils for National Defense, created by the federal government to support the war (WWI) effort, as well as from religious groups and the trade union auxiliaries. By May 1919, the Brooklyn Tenant Union (BTU), one of the first tenant advocacy groups, had many of its 4,000 members ready to withhold their rents until increases were rolled back. To make their case, they barricaded themselves into apartments, made speeches from tenement windows, and threatened to pour boiling water on anyone who tried to evict them.

In 1922, the New York Women's Trade Union League (NYW-TUL) founded the Housewives' Industrial League, which called for a public investigation into the health, housing, and other conditions of non-wage-earning women in the home. Mothers in the Communist Party created the United Council of Working-Class Wives to support workplace strikes but soon focussed on the cost of food, fuel, housing, education, and other social welfare issues. Their activities attracted large numbers of non-party women. That same year, the New England Conference of Working-Class Women, representing forty-eight organizations, pledged to fight not only for lower food prices, but also for maternity insurance and an end to child labor.

The collapse of the economy in 1929 led to a new round of community activism. Working-class women found various ways to protect their families from the ravages of the Depression. In rural communities, they exchanged skills, services, clothing, and food, while in urban areas, they began to demand state action. Building on existing networks, housewives in Jewish, Polish, Finnish, Swedish, Irish, Slavic, and African-American communities once again supported strikes, organized consumer boycotts, and blocked evictions. One of the largest consumer actions took place in 1935, when housewives boycotted butcher shops in many large cities, closing some 4,500 in New York City alone. Black working-class women formed their own Housewives' Leagues, launched "Don't Buy Where You Can't Work" campaigns in Baltimore, Chicago, Cleveland, Detroit, New York City, and Washington, D.C., and demanded 75,000 jobs for blacks who had lost theirs during the Depression. In the South, black women joined the 10,000-member interracial Southern Tenant Farmers' Union, which was founded in Arkansas to resist the evictions that began when the Agricultural Adjustment Act paid farmers to destroy crops in order to increase prices. In the end, these "cost-of-living" protests galvanized women in Chicago, Cleveland, Detroit, Los Angeles, Milwaukee, Minneapolis, Newark, Philadelphia, Patterson, St. Louis, Missouri, and Seattle—to name just a few of the places they rose up angry.

In some cities, the uprisings were shortlived. In others, they led to sophisticated organizations—most notably, the Detroit Women's League Against the High Cost of Living, the Chicago United Council Against the High Cost of Living, and the Women's Work Committee of the Washington Commonwealth Federation. The United Council of Working-Class Wives was formed in June 1929 and by 1931 had forty-eight branches in New York City alone. In 1937, as the Depression deepened, its successor, the Progressive Women's Council, led 3,000 women in sit-ins at New York City's twenty-nine largest relief centers, demanding

Depression-era demonstrators for unemployment insurance. [Culver Pictures]

a 40 percent increase in benefits, a cash allowance for clothing, and twenty-four-hour service for emergency cases. This housewife activism peaked in an explosion of protests in the early 1940s after Roosevelt cut social spending in response to conservative critics.[26] The advent of World War II led to a suspension of protest, but huge price increases of 1946-1947 and 1951 sparked two of the largest consumer strikes in U.S. history.

The housewives' movement was a national phenomenon in which women politicized the home, the family, and motherhood in unprecedented ways. They increasingly put pressure on the government to regulate the meat and milk industries, to provide decent and affordable housing, and to give them the heath, education, and welfare services they felt they needed to fulfill their gendered obligations. On the one hand, this activism perpetuated women's traditional roles. On the other hand, however,

by holding both the system of production and the state responsible for meeting basic human needs, it implicitly endorsed a
more radical vision of how society should work.

A WOMAN'S WORK IS NEVER DONE: ACTIVISM
AFTER WORLD WAR II

Contrary to popular wisdom, middle- and working-class
women remained active after World War II. By this time, however, the "welfare state economy" had begun to shape their
efforts. Although virulently anti-government, anti-communist,
and anti-feminist attitudes limited what they could accomplish,
between 1945 and 1960 many women worked in peace, civil
rights, religious, and other organizations. They increasingly held
the government responsible for correcting social conditions.[27]
One group of women's organizations clustered around the National Women's Party (NWP), which had been founded during
the suffrage battle and was the only national women's rights
group that remained active in this period. Although the organization shrank dramatically, and became marginalized because it harbored racist, anti-Semitic, and right-wing leanings, it
nonetheless continued to press Congress to support an Equal
Rights Amendment (ERA), which it had first introduced in 1921.

The second, and much larger, postwar group of women's organizations was allied to the Women's Bureau of the Department
of Labor. From the Business and Professional Women to the United
Auto Workers' Women's Bureau, these reform-oriented women
considered feminism too narrowly focused on women's rights, at
the expense of working-class women's concerns. They actively
opposed the ERA during the 1940s and 1950s, fearing that it would
undercut labor laws that protected employed women. Instead, they
continued to argue for pay equity, improved working conditions,
and special protection for women on the job.

A third group, closely connected to the second, included women
who became active in the Democratic and Republican parties, each
of which had a women's division. By the 1950s, women were the

backbone of both local and national electoral activity, but they were still locked out of major decision-making roles. Among many other activities, therefore, the women's divisions and their supporters fought to place women in top policymaking posts. They hoped that by presenting lists of qualified women to party leaders, supporting women who were running for elected office, and organizing women into a political constituency, they would improve the status of all women and help transform society.

A fourth group was made up of African-American women. Often unrecognized outside their own communities because the women's movement remained effectively segregated, these women continued to work on issues of central concern to them.

They also played key leadership roles in the civil rights movement. They worked with the National Council of Negro Women, the National Association of Colored Women, and black sororities to protest racial discrimination, although, like white women, they were divided over the ERA, with the National Association of Colored Women in favor and the National Council of Negro Women opposed. They played a major behind-the-scenes role in the Southern Christian Leadership Conference, the church-based organization formed by Martin Luther King, Jr., in 1957, and although they received little credit at the time, it was the Women's Political Council of Montgomery, Alabama, a group of professional black women, that organized the historic Montgomery bus boycott. The 381-day protest—triggered when Rosa Parks, a department store seamstress and secretary of the Alabama NAACP, was arrested for refusing to move to the back of bus—became a critical event in the postwar civil rights struggle.[28] Many black women who later became nationally known leaders started out as local civil rights activists in the late 1950s and early 1960s.[29] They assisted the Freedom Riders, were central to the movement to desegregate public accommodations,[30] and organized voter registration drives, including the one in Mississippi that led to the formation of the Mississippi Freedom Democratic Party (MFDP). Headed by Fannie Lou Hamer, the MFDP delegation to the 1964 Democratic National Convention not only successfully challenged the party but elected the first black legislator in a Southern state. Black women students joined the first sit-ins in the 1960s—a strategy that became the guiding philosophy of the Student Nonviolent Coordinating Committee (SNCC)—and later they created the Black Women's Liberation Committee within SNCC (1964).[31]

In the mid-1960s, white women broke away from the gradualism that characterized the major political parties and the mainstream women's groups to form new feminist organizations, including the National Organization of Women (1967), the Women's Equity Action League (1968), and the National Women's Political Caucus (1971).[32] These "second wave" feminists demanded that the government outlaw sex discrimination and enforce equal rights in employment, education, and healthcare. They also targeted welfare state benefits, and won a minimum wage for domestic workers, greater access to education, admission to most military academies, job protection for pregnant workers, and a woman's right to receive credit on the basis of her own record. It was winning the right to abortion, however, that gave the greatest impetus to the new feminist movement.

In addition, younger, more militant, and mostly white women in the SNCC and Students for a Democratic Society (SDS) began to resist male domination in their organizations and personal lives, and to call for women's *liberation,* not just women's *rights.*[33] This insurgency, which crossed race, class, and age lines, led to the creation of the National Conference of Puerto Rican Women (1972), the National Black Feminist Organization (1973), the National Alliance of Black Feminists (1973), the Mexican American Women's Association (1974), the Coalition of Labor Union Women (1974), and the Older Women's League (1980). Each organization targeted its own constituency, however, and the women's movement has continued to be plagued by race, class, and other tensions.

The tumultuous climate of the late 1960s and early 1970s also sparked activism among working-class housewives and single mothers on welfare. In city after city, community-based women began to revive the effort to improve their standard of living. Black, Latina, and white housewives fought against bank redlining and toxic waste dumps, and for rent control, social services, better schools, and safe streets. In the mid-1970s, when fiscal cutbacks threatened neighborhood services, working-class women mobilized against clinic and hospital closings, and demanded better funding for schools. The Congress of Neighborhood Women, founded in 1974 and one of the better-known groups of working-class women, has continued its work.

EARLY WELFARE RIGHTS ORGANIZING: THE NATIONAL WELFARE RIGHTS ORGANIZATION

In the 1960s, women on welfare also began to organize in their own interests.[34] Drawing on the long tradition of informal support networks, especially in the black community, these women redefined welfare as a right rather than a privilege, and fought to obtain the benefits to which they were entitled by law. Just as workers employed in factories had discovered their common plight and formed unions to gain strength in numbers, so being "on welfare" provided a basis for women to join forces to protest their meager benefits and the system's controlling rules. While client protest against the welfare system was not new, the welfare rights movement that grew out of these local efforts turned out to be the most significant social protest by poor people since World War II.

The conditions of the mid-1960s—economic prosperity, a liberal political climate, active social movements, political uprisings, and a national war on poverty—created a space in which women on welfare could organize.[35] By this time, the Southern civil rights movement had all but ended and many activists had turned their efforts Northward, drawn by incipient political stirrings among the black urban masses. The 1963 March on Washington and the 1964 War on Poverty focused national attention on economic as well as civil rights issues, as did the twenty-one major riots and civil disorders in 1966, and eighty-three in 1967. The War on Poverty's Community Action Program provided legal and counseling services that helped poor women assert their rights, and with the help of VISTA volunteers, nuns, priests, ministers, and social workers, it facilitated the formation of local welfare rights groups.

The convergence of these forces led George Wiley, a black chemistry professor from Syracuse University and former associate director of the Congress of Racial Equality (CORE), along with other mostly male veterans of the civil rights movement, to form a national welfare rights organization. Its program was based on "A Strategy to End Poverty," a paper written by two academically based social activists, Frances Fox Piven and Richard A. Cloward, that proposed flooding the welfare system with applicants and demands for benefits. Piven and Cloward argued that at least half the families entitled to AFDC never applied, while many others were turned away. They pointed out that welfare departments kept women on welfare uninformed of the range of benefits to which they were entitled, including special grants for clothing and household items, and that if women insisted on what was theirs by law, many more would receive needed financial aid. The resulting surge of applications would also create a fiscal crisis for welfare departments and a political crisis for the Democratic Party. The demand for more welfare dollars would lead big-city Democratic coalitions to split over how to use urban resources and would force the national Democratic Party to put forward a federal solution to poverty that involved the redistribution of income toward the poor.

The formation of a national movement was preceded by growing activity at the local level. In 1963, Johnnie Tillmon, a welfare mother of five, organized Mothers Anonymous in Watts, California; other women formed the Alameda County, California, Welfare Rights organization. The Minneapolis AFDC League, founded in 1964, grew out of a single parents' group at the local YWCA. In 1965, agitation by poor women against welfare cuts led to the Ohio Steering Committee for Adequate Welfare, and in 1966 the Brooklyn Action Welfare Council (B-WAC) was organized after some women attended a welfare rights planning meeting in Washington, D.C. Within a year after the conference, storefront welfare rights centers existed in almost every low-income Brooklyn community. In June 1966, Ohio welfare rights groups staged a 155-mile "Walk for Adequate Welfare" from Cleveland to the state capital in Columbus. National welfare rights planners, led by Wiley, turned this local march into a national media event. They mobilized support for the forty people who set out from Cleveland and for the 5,000 or so others who joined them for some part of the ten-day march. On the last day, simultaneous demonstrations were held in twenty-four cities nationwide, giving official birth to the national welfare rights movement.

In August 1967, the National Welfare Rights Organization (NWRO) held its first national convention, attended by 175 people from forty-five cities in twenty-one states. An organizational structure was set up and Johnnie Tillmon was elected chair. George Wiley, who had earlier been chosen as national director, had already opened the first field office in Washington, D.C. By the time of the convention, the NWRO had 5,000 dues-paying members, concentrated in New York, California, Pennsylvania, Michigan, Virginia, Massachusetts, Ohio, New Jersey, and Illinois. Using a grassroots organizing strategy, it expanded its membership to 22,000 by 1969. The number of local WRO's grew as well, from 130 in twenty-three states in 1966 to 900 in fifty states in 1971.

The NWRO had two main aims: to improve public assistance and to establish a federally guaranteed income. Its organizing strategies ranged from solving individual grievances to collective agitation at welfare offices. Its strategy contributed to the welfare "explosion" of the late 1960s (described in Part 2), and it mounted a militant counteroffensive to welfare cuts in cities in California, New York, Massachusetts, Minnesota, Nevada, New Jersey, and Wisconsin, many of which drew the police and led to arrests. In addition, it lobbied against forced work programs, suitable-home policies, and man-in-the-house rules. Its work transferred millions of dollars to the poor and attracted thousands of women to the welfare rights movement.

Despite positive media coverage and success in mobilizing women across the nation, the NWRO was forced to shift from a street strategy to a political strategy as the times changed. Funding became harder to come by, liberal support diminished, the leadership was co-opted by both politicians and welfare agencies, and the general political climate was more conservative. The organization turned to lobbying against Nixon's Family Assistance Plan (1969-1971), working with local welfare departments to bring about change, and applying for government grants. None of this worked, and in 1975 it declared bankruptcy and closed its doors.

WELFARE BECOMES A WOMEN'S ISSUE

The welfare rights movement did not disappear, however, for it had created a sense of entitlement and a cadre of politicized and battle-tested women who were willing to work to keep the cause alive. Moreover, in the mid-1970s a new generation of welfare rights groups arose. Unlike the first wave, which was composed mainly of black women and pursued the politics of class, the second wave included increasing numbers of white women, whose standard of living had fallen due to rising divorce rates and low wages.[36] Influenced by the women's liberation movement, women on welfare—both white women and women of color—began to see welfare as a matter of gender as well as economics.

The first sign of this new wave of activity was in 1972, when the NWRO's women leaders wrested control of the organization from Wiley, forcing him to resign, and made Johnnie Tillmon the executive director. In 1974, white feminists organized the Downtown Welfare Rights Action Center (D-WAC) in New York City. Influenced by feminism, its members (along with groups in New Jersey and elsewhere) argued that welfare was a women's issue because so few jobs with decent pay were available to women and because there was so little affordable childcare. More and more white women attended the NWRO's

1974 and 1977 conventions, including young feminists identified with the feminist *and* the welfare rights movements.

The more established feminist groups had played a very minor role in the earlier welfare rights movement, but in the early 1970s the National Organization of Women (NOW), the Women's Equity Action League (WEAL), and the Women's Lobby began to take note of poverty. While the majority of women in NOW remained indifferent or resistant, NOW chapters in New Mexico, California, Minnesota, and Maryland made limited overtures to the NWRO as part of an effort to address poor women's issues.[37] A few black feminist groups, such as the National Black Feminist Organization and the Coalition of 100 Black Women, also established loose ties with the NWRO. In 1976, some mainstream women's groups, as well as the Coalition of Labor Union Women, the National Congress of Neighborhood Women, and Housewives for the ERA, took a stand against Carter's welfare reform bill because it failed to value women's work at home and because it did not provide for childcare so that a woman could choose to work in *or* outside the home without penalty. In 1977, the National Council of Women, Work, and Welfare—a coalition that came out of the welfare rights movement— also attempted to mobilize political support for welfare as a women's issue.

These efforts on the part of middle-class feminist groups came too late to significantly influence the welfare reform debate, however, especially since a backlash against the War on Poverty and the 1960s social movements was underway. The effort was in any case difficult because feminists and the NRWO disagreed on some basic issues. First, many feminists supported government work programs as a way to help women move out of the home. In contrast, the NWRO saw this as forced labor that prevented women from choosing where—home or market— they wanted to work. On another front, most feminist groups of the 1970s were devoting considerable resources to the ERA, which ranked low on the NWRO's priority list because it would do away with protective labor laws. On the other hand, the

NWRO male leadership believed that poor women needed husbands rather than economic independence through work; this not only alienated nearly all feminists but was eventually disavowed by the women leaders of NWRO as well.

The attack on social programs by the Reagan administration in the 1980s spawned another round of welfare rights activism, this time shaped by the "austerity economy." On June 30, 1987, the twenty-first anniversary of NWRO's founding, welfare mothers and organizers formed the National Welfare Rights Union (NWRU). With leadership from the earlier movement, as well as ties to other poor people's groups, the NWRU dedicated itself "to the pursuit of social justice for all members of our society, particularly those who have been excluded from the benefits of this nation."[38] Its first annual convention, in September 1988, drew over 100 people from eighteen states. In July 1989, over 350 people attended a National Survival Summit in Philadelphia organized by the NRWU, the National Union of the Homeless, and the National Anti-Hunger Coalition. The participants agreed to organize state survival summits and a national "Up and Out of Poverty, Now!" campaign, to be led by people who themselves lived in poverty. Subsequent survival summits have targeted youth, hunger, homelessness, poor women, media blackouts of poor people's activism, and, of course, the renewed drive to reform welfare.

Like their predecessors, the NWRU and its allies took on the practices of local welfare offices on the one hand and national policy on the other. NWRU members frequently "turned up the street heat" by staging militant actions, including civil disobedience. They organized "No Heat, No Peace" sit-ins at a Michigan welfare office, a lengthy "No Housing, No Peace" takeover of empty houses owned by the Department of Housing and Urban Development in New York City and Salt Lake City, Utah, and tent cities in Michigan and New York. The Philadelphia-based Kensington Welfare Rights Union appropriated an abandoned building and turned it into a community center in a neighborhood that had none, while the NWRU chapter in Oakland, California, agitated long and hard against that state's punitive welfare policies.

Nationally, the NWRU regularly holds conferences where women (and men) on welfare from around the country are trained as activists. The NWRU opposed the 1988 Family Support Act, Clinton's 1994 welfare reform bill, the January 1995 Republican Contract With America, and the 1995 House and Senate welfare reform bills. At its July 1994 "Who Speaks for the Poor?" conference, it announced a four-part organizing, legislative, public relations, and legal strategy to combat these welfare reform efforts.[39] That same year, the "Up and Out of Poverty, Now!" campaign mobilized poor women and their supporters for a tax-day protest in fifteen cities across the United States and Canada. In 1995, the NWRU, along with the rest of the welfare advocacy community, demanded that Clinton veto any welfare reform legislation that came out of Congress.

The growing welfare rights network includes long-standing welfare rights groups, such as the Coalition for Basic Human Needs in Massachusetts; Parents for Justice in New Hampshire; the Welfare Warriors in Milwaukee; Empower in Rochester, New York; The Reform Organization of Welfare in St. Louis; Women for Economic Security in Chicago; the Women's Union in Vermont; and Arise in Springfield, Massachusetts. It also includes groups formed in the late 1980s and early 1990s, such as the Welfare Warriors in Long Island, New York; JEDI Women (Justice, Economic Dignity and Independence for Women) in Salt Lake City, Utah; and the Women's Economic Agenda Project (WEAP) in Oakland, California. Welfare reform activism has cropped up on many college campuses, as local, state, and national welfare cutbacks and stricter mandatory work programs make it nearly impossible for welfare recipients to complete their college education. News of all these efforts rarely makes it into the mainstream press, but is regularly reported in *Survival News* (published in Boston) and the *Welfare Mothers' Voice* (published in Milwaukee), both of which are written by and for welfare mothers, as well as in many smaller organizational newsletters. Although federal priorities have certainly not been turned around, women on welfare are on the move and, in some states, have managed to limit some of the worst welfare reforms.

Following the lead of the groups that formed in the 1970s, some of newer groups are organizing women on welfare self-consciously *as women*. The names of their organizations—Women for Economic Security; the Women's Union; Justice, Independence, and Dignity for Women; and Women's Economic Agenda—reflect this. Although they worked at first at the local level, they have recently begun to connect nationally. For instance, the Oakland-based WEAP convened over 400 poor women in 1992 for the first ever Poor Women's Convention; their theme, "Under Attack but Fighting Back" inspired the title of this book. The meeting was the first chance many of the women had had to leave their communities and discover that other women lived exactly as they did. The following week, a group of women who had attended the convention joined with 200 other poor women at the San Francisco Hilton to let Governor Pete Wilson, who was holding a fundraiser, know what they thought of his welfare ideas. After the governor refused to meet with them, eleven of the women sat down in the hotel lobby. The arrest of the "Hilton 11" hit the network news, and viewers heard one women cry out, "I'm getting arrested for wanting to feed my kids."[40] On Valentine's Day 1995, under JEDI leadership, welfare rights groups in seventy-seven cities in thirty-eight states mounted local actions and sent thousands of postcards to local and state legislators, reminding them that "Our children's hearts are in your hands." This network was also mobilized to join the campaign to get Clinton to veto all punitive welfare legislation.

The NWRU and other welfare rights groups have also made overtures to middle-class women's organizations, recognizing that it is important for poor women to build bridges across class and race lines. While only a beginning, women's groups in and outside of the feminist community have caught up with Johnnie Tillmon, who back in 1972 pointed out how welfare is a women's issue: "There's one good thing about welfare. It kills your illusions about yourself, and about where this society is really at. It's laid out for you straight. You have to learn to fight, to be aggressive, or you just don't make it. If you can survive long enough on welfare, you can survive anything. It gives you a kind of freedom, a sense of your own power and togetherness with other women."[41]

NOW responded positively when the NWRU invited it to become a member of its "Up and Out of Poverty, Now!" campaign. In 1992, NOW invited NWRU President Marion Kramer to address its annual convention and went on to recommend that all local branches find ways to support the poor women's organizations in their areas. NOW also voted not to endorse any political candidate who called for harsh welfare reforms. Patricia Ireland, president of NOW, went on record against welfare reform and, along with Marion Kramer, was arrested trying to gain entry to a Congressional hearing on the issue. NOW intensified its commitment to welfare rights at its 1994 convention, where it launched an emergency national campaign, called "As If Women Matter," to generate opposition to the welfare reforms that were then emanating from both state legislatures and Congress, and to promote nonpunitive solutions for "ending poverty as we know it."[42] NOW's "100 Days of Action" campaign against the Contract With America culminated in an April 1995 mass rally in Washington, D.C., where NOW expanded the definition of violence against women—the theme of the rally—to include poverty and punitive welfare reform.

In varying degrees, other feminist groups have also joined the welfare rights movement. The NOW Legal Defense and Education Fund (which is not part of NOW) was one of the first feminist organizations to do the hard work of bringing welfare mothers, anti-poverty advocates, and feminists into the same room. It also helped organize eighty groups into the Child Exclusion Coalition, which included leading feminist, reproductive rights, religious, and right-to-life organizations. For very different reasons, each of these groups strongly opposed any welfare reform that denied aid to children born while their mothers are on AFDC. The Institute for Women's Policy Research, Wider Opportunities for Women, the Center for Reproductive Law and Policy, the National Black Women's Health Project, the American Civil Liberties Union's Reproductive Rights Project, among other groups, have put opposition to punitive welfare reform on their agendas.

Some organizations with large female memberships but not necessarily feminist programs have also begun to see that welfare reform affects women (and children). In Spring 1995, the *Women's Initiative Network* newsletter, published by the American Association of Retired Persons (AARP), warned that welfare reform was a testing ground for changes in entitlement programs that "would be a disaster for mid-life and older women"[43] who depend heavily on Medicaid, Medicare, Supplemental Security Income, and public housing, or who raise grandchildren with the help of AFDC. It added that the stereotypes used to justify cutting senior citizen programs—that the elderly are "greedy geezers" who do not need government aid or "undeserving" people who use public benefits instead of saving for their old age—are not unlike the myths used to demonize welfare mothers, and that such threats ultimately harm everyone.

In 1994 and 1995, as Congress considered various welfare reform bills, many women academics and professionals lent their names and expertise to efforts to refute the myths behind welfare reform. A noted in Part 1, in 1994 a group of seventy-six scholars (male and female) issued a press release that stated that the existing research contained little or no evidence of a relationship between welfare and a woman's childbearing decisions. Individual women have also conducted research, appeared on radio and TV, written op-ed pieces, and made themselves available to local groups fighting welfare reform. On several occasions when Congress seemed on the brink of passing a reform bill, women's groups have mobilized nationwide opposition. In the fall of 1994, for instance, more than 750 women academics issued a statement—printed in the *New York Review of Books* and the *New Republic*—that opposed Clinton's plan. On August 8, 1995, the Committee of One Hundred Women, joined by many other women's, labor, and professional groups, ran a full-page ad in the *New York Times* that explained "Why Every Woman in

America Should Beware of Welfare Cuts" and declared that "A War Against Poor Women Is a War Against All Women!" Drawing on its roster of well-established artists, authors, politicians, professionals, academics, and activists, the Committee of One Hundred Women has lobbied intensively against Congressional welfare bills, organized press conferences, and conducted vigils outside the White House. In December 1995, the National Association of Social Workers, the majority of whose members are women, collected several thousand signatures for still another *New York Times* ad directed at Clinton. Supporting the national Veto Campaign, it stated, "Don't Sign Any Welfare Bill That Abandons the Nation's Children." The Council of Presidents (of national women's organizations), which represents 6 million women and ninety women's organizations, developed a "Women's Pledge on Welfare Reform" to organize opposition to welfare reform among feminist professional and advocacy groups. If they can be sustained and developed, these efforts at solidarity among women of different classes and races holds some promise for building a base for a more progressive social welfare policy in the future.

WHAT CAN THE FUTURE HOLD?

If the current welfare reform bills succeed in turning AFDC into state-administered block grants, we will have come full circle, back to the social welfare structures that existed before the 1935 Social Security Act required the federal government to guarantee public assistance to the poor. The first order of business, therefore, is to save AFDC as a federalized program, raise the grant to at least the poverty level, provide women with child and healthcare services, and eliminate punitive measures designed to control their work and family behavior.

But in addition to defending AFDC against the current assault, welfare rights advocates have tried to envision better alternatives. While some of the proposals hope to improve welfare in the short run, others are more far-reaching plans to secure economic independence for women. For instance, Barbara Bergmann and Heidi Hartmann, two nationally known economists and co-chairs of the Economists' Policy Group for Women's Issues, have developed a plan to help women within the framework of what they believe might be tolerated in today's conservative political climate. Called Help for Working Parents (HWP), it stresses work as the means to economic independence, and argues for moving poor parents out of poverty by providing childcare, healthcare, and housing assistance—all regardless of a woman's marital status. HWP would reward work by supplementing minimum-wage jobs with noncash benefits and by expanding the Earned Income Tax Credit. For instance, a single mother with two children who worked full-time at the minimum wage would receive about $24,500 a year, double the 1994 poverty level of income for a family of three. Single parents not in paid jobs would receive a series of vouchers each month, including Food Stamps and $100 in cash. The HWP program would cost much more than the $25 billion currently spent on AFDC, but would also provide a far better way to help women who work.[44]

Nancy Fraser, a professor of philosophy and research fellow at the Center for Urban Affairs and Policy at Northwestern University, has a less immediately pragmatic vision that emphasizes the importance of women's caretaking work and allows women to choose between home and market. Fraser would make the labor market more women-friendly through the provision of better childcare, eldercare, and other services; an end to sex discrimination, sexual harassment, and other obstacles to equal employment; and the creation of permanent, full-time, well-paid jobs. She would also upgrade existing social insurance plans to take women's labor market needs in account. In recognition of caretaking as socially valuable work, she proposes "caregiver parity"—i.e., a caregiver allowance to compensate women for the work of bearing and raising children, for housework, and for other socially necessary domestic labor. The caregiver allowance would support a family at the same level as a breadwinner's wage, and be combined with flextime, family leave, and other policies to make the workplace more accessible to caretakers. Fraser also integrates breadwinner and caregiver benefits into a single system so that, for example, a women finishing a spell of supported caregiving but unable to find market work and a laid-off factory worker in the same situation would both become eligible for Unemployment Insurance. She adds another need-based, means-tested benefit for those unable to do either waged or caregiving work.[45]

Ann Orloff, a professor of sociology at the University of Wisconsin, has developed a plan that specifically targets the gender relations of power.[46] This more radical reform is based on the belief that women need programs that will enhance their autonomy and permit them to escape both market exploitation and male domination, and that if social policy is to help women it must go beyond promoting women's work, covering the costs of social reproduction, and easing caretaking burdens to freeing them from the need to enter into potentially oppressive relationships of any kind. The programs Orloff proposes would provide women with access to independent incomes in order to insulate them from exploitation in the labor market and free them from depending on marriage for economic support. To be women-friendly, such programs would make it possible for women to form and maintain households without having to marry and would increase the standard of living in such women-maintained homes.

Martha Fineman, a professor at Columbia University School of Law, goes one step further and calls for an end to the legal basis of marriage (but not necessarily the relationship itself), the elimination of all government subsidies and protection designed uphold this institution, *and* the recognition that nurturing units—i.e., caregiving families, whatever their shape or structure—are inevitably dependent and may require some type of government support.[47]

Speaking for welfare mothers themselves, the National Welfare Rights Union called for replacing welfare with a guaranteed annual income, echoing various components of other feminist plans. Their manifesto states:

Members of the Kensington Welfare Rights Union in Philadelphia protest against human service proposals, 1995. [Harvey Finkle/ Impact Visuals]

All people should have an adequate income whether from benefits or from jobs that pay enough to live on, a guaranteed annual income so that no one in this nation need live in poverty. All people should be able to live a life of dignity with full freedom and respect for human rights.... All women who want to work outside the home should have the opportunity to earn a wage that will allow them to meet all the needs of their families. We also respect the right of all women who chose to stay in the home and nurture their children. They should be fully supported in their task for the important contribution that they are making to society.[48]

In these harsh times, we need to dream while we struggle to protect poor women and AFDC. It is imperative that we question existing programs and invent alternatives, even if these at first seem outrageous. In the end, this will help us come to terms with a future in which there may not be enough paid work or adequate incomes for everyone, but in which people will still need a decent standard of living and caregiving work will still need to be done. Faced with these realities, instead of debating the relative merits of income support vs. employment policies, as often happens today, we need to develop the best policies we can on *both* fronts. Fraser has five gender-sensitive objectives that could be used to assess such future reforms: social welfare programs should (1) prevent poverty, (2) prohibit the exploitation of vulnerable people, (3) reduce gender, race, and class inequalities, (4) promote women's full participation in society on par with men and persons of color on par with whites, and (5) restructure government programs, along with other social institutions designed primarily for white men, so that women can fully benefit from them.[49] If these guidelines were to be followed, welfare "as we know it" would be replaced by a responsive welfare state in a society based on justice and equality for all.

As this book has tried to show, achieving this will require pressure from below. In the words of Frederick Douglass, abolitionist and supporter of women's rights, "Power concedes nothing without a demand." And as women activists have always known, we must dare to struggle if we expect to win!

NOTES

PART 1: UNDER ATTACK: WOMEN AND WELFARE REFORM TODAY

1. Bill Clinton and Al Gore, *Putting People First: How We Can All Change America*, cited in "Charge to the Working Group on Welfare Reform, Family Support and Independence." This group was formed by President Clinton in June 1993 to develop his welfare reform plan and chaired by David Ellwood and Bruce Reed.
2. Jan Hagen and Liane Davis, *Another Perspective on Welfare Reform: Conversations With Mothers on Welfare* (Nelson A. Rockefeller Institute of Government, SUNY, Albany, NY, 1994, Monograph), p. 38.
3. Linda Gordon, *Pitied But Not Entitled: Single Mothers and the History of Welfare* (New York: Free Press, 1994), p. 1.
4. Samuel Bowles, "The Crisis of Liberal Democratic Capitalism," *Politics and Society* 11 (1982): 51-93; Samuel Bowles, David Gordon, and Thomas Weisskopf, *Beyond the Wasteland: A Democratic Alternative to Economic Decline* (Garden City, NY: Anchor/Doubleday, 1983); Bowles, Gordon, and Weisskopf, "Power and Profits: The Social Structure of Accumulation and the Profitability of the Post-War U.S. Economy," *Review of Radical Economics* 1 & 2 (1986): 32-167; Fred Block, "Rethinking the Political Economy of the Welfare State," in *The Mean Season: The Attack on the Welfare State*, ed. Fred

Block, Richard A. Cloward, Barbara Ehrenreich, and Francis Fox Piven (New York: Pantheon, 1987), pp. 109-160.

5. Congressional Budget Office, *Reducing Entitlement Spending* (Washington, D.C.: Government Printing Office, 1994), Table 1, p. x.

6. American Enterprise Institute, "A Community of Self-Reliance: A New Consensus on Family and Welfare" (Washington, D.C.: American Enterprise Institute, 1987, Report), p. 4; Robert Rector, "Combatting Family Disintegration, Crime and Dependence: Welfare Reform and Beyond," *Heritage Foundation Backgrounder* (Newsletter), 8 April 1994, p. 7.

7. White House Working Group on the Family, "The Family: Preserving America's Future" (Department of Education, Office of the Under Secretary, 13 November 1986, Press release and report), p. 21; Michael Tanner, "Ending Welfare As We Know It," *Policy Analysis* 212 (7 July 1994): 22-23; Charles Murray, "The Emerging White Underclass and How to Save It," *Philadelphia Inquirer,* 15 November 1993, p. A15.

8. See, for example, Paul M. Sweezy, *The Theory of Capitalist Development* (New York: Monthly Review Press, 1968), pp. 239-53.

9. See, for example, Gosta Epsing-Anderson, *Three Worlds of Welfare Capitalism* (Princeton, NJ: Princeton University Press, 1990); Epsing-Anderson, *Politics Against Markets: The Social Democratic Road to Power* (Princeton, NJ: Princeton University Press, 1985); Frances Fox Piven and Richard A. Cloward, *The New Class War: Reagan's Attack on the Welfare State and Its Consequences* (New York: Pantheon Books, 1982), p. 118.

10. Richard May, "1993 Poverty and Income Trends" (Washington, D.C.: Center on Budget and Policy Priorities, March 1995, Report), p. 11.

11. House Committee on Ways and Means, *Overview of Entitlement Programs, 1994 Green Book* (Washington, D.C.: Government Printing Office, 1994), p. 398, 399, 1255.

12. LRA's Economic Notes 63, no. 12 (December 1995): 4.

13. House Committee on Ways and Means, *Overview of Entitlement Programs, 1994 Green Book,* p. 389; Robert Pear, "Welfare and Food Stamp Rolls End Six Years of Increases," *New York Times,* 14 March 1995, p. 18; Center for Law and Social Policy, "AFDC Caseload Declines: Implications for Block Grant Planning" (Washington, D.C., 2 October 1995, Factsheet), p. 1.

14. Labor Institute, *Corporate Power and the American Dream* (New York: Labor Institute, April 1995).

15. Jason DeParle, "Census Sees Falling Income and More Poor," *New York Times,* 7 October 1994, p. A13.

16. Aaron Bernstein, "Where the Jobs Are, the Skills Aren't," *Business Week,* 19 September 1988, p. 108; Department of Labor, *WorkForce 2000: Work and Workers for the 21st Century* (Washington, D.C.: Government Printing Office, 1987).

17. National Alliance of Business, *Employment Policies: Looking to the Year 2000* (Washington, D.C., February 1986), pp. i, 8.

18. American Enterprise Institute, "A Community of Self-Reliance," p. 11.

19. Katherine S. Newman, "What Inner City Jobs for Welfare Moms?" *New York Times,* 20 May 1995, p. 23.

20. Jodie Levin-Epstein, "Clinton Welfare Options Under Consideration," *States*

Update: A CLASP Report on State Welfare Reform Developments (Washington, D.C.: Center for Law and Social Policy (CLASP), 23 December 1993), pp. 1-2.

21. Center on Social Welfare Policy and Law, "Preliminary Analysis of Title I of H.R. 4, As Passed by the Senate on September 9/95" (Washington, D.C., 26 September 1995, Short brief), pp. 5-6; Mark Greenberg, "Understanding the Clinton Welfare Bill: Two Years and Work" (Washington, D.C.: Center For Law and Social Policy (CLASP), 12 July 1994, Short brief), pp. 1-15; Robin Toner, "Senate Approves Welfare Plan That Would End Guarantee," *New York Times*, 20 September 1995, p. 1.

22. Fordice quoted in Kevin Sack, "In Mississippi, Will Poor Grow Poorer with State Welfare Plan," *New York Times*, 23 October 1995, p. A1; Lawrence M. Mead, *The New Politics of Poverty* (New York: Basic Books, 1992), p. 12; Rector quoted in Center on Social Welfare Policy and Law, "Welfare Reform Hearings: January 1995" (Washington, D.C., 8 February 1995, Short brief), p. 1.

23. Irene Skricki, "Unheard Voices: Participants Evaluate the JOBS Program" (Washington, D.C.: Coalition on Human Needs, January 1993, Report), p. 13.

24. April quoted in Jane Collins and Donna Southwell, *Life on the Edge: The Stories of Seven Massachusetts Women on Welfare* (Boston: Massachusetts Human Service Coalition, 1994), p. 13; Hagen and Davis, "Another Perspective on Welfare Reform," p. 12.

25. LaDonna Pavetti, "The Dynamics of Welfare and Work: Exploring the Process by Which Young Women Work Their Way Off Welfare," cited in House Committee on Ways and Means, *Overview of Entitlement Programs, 1994 Green Book*, pp. 441-42.

26. Roberta Spalter-Roth, Beverly Burr, Heidi Hartmann, and Lois Shaw, "Welfare That Works: The Working Lives of AFDC Recipients" (Washington, D.C.: Institute For Women's Policy Research, 20 March 1995, Report), pp. 40, 43-44.

27. Ibid., p. 1, 43.

28. Jan Hagen and Irene Lurie, *Implementing JOBS: Progress and Promise* (Albany, NY: Nelson A. Rockefeller Institute of Government, August 1994, Monograph), p. 230; Robert Moffitt, *Incentive Effects of the U.S. Welfare System: A Review*, Institute for Research on Poverty Special Report, No. 48 (Madison, WI: Institute for Research on Poverty, University of Wisconsin-Madison, March 1991, Monograph); James Riccio and Daniel Friedlander, "GAIN: Program Strategies, Participation, Patterns and First-Year Impact in Six Counties" (New York: Manpower Demonstration Research Corporation, May 1992, Report); Government Accounting Office, *Welfare to Work: States Begin JOBS, but Fiscal and Other Problems May Impede Their Progress* (Washington, D.C.: Government Printing Office, September 1992), p. 43.

29. Lawrence Mishel and John Schmitt, "Cutting Wages by Cutting Welfare: The Impact of Reform on the Low-Wage Labor Market" (Washington, D.C.: Economic Policy Institute, 1995, Report).

30. Spalter-Roth, Burr, Hartmann, and Shaw, "Welfare That Works," p. 59.

31. Hunger Action Network of New York State, *Newsletter*, 15 February 1995, p. 8; Jonathan Rabinowitz, "Welfare Fallout Traps Mothers: Plan Threatens Education," *New York Times*, 19 May 1995, p. B1; Skricki, "Unheard Voices," p. 13.

32. Christopher Jencks, "What Is the Underclass—and Is It Growing?" *Focus* 12, no. 1 (Spring/Summer 1989): 21.

33. White House Working Group on the Family, "The Family: Preserving America's Future," p. 33.

34. Department of Health and Human Services, *Characteristics and Financial Circumstances of AFDC Recipients* (Washington, D.C.: Government Printing Office, 1992), Table 16.

35. Because anti-abortion groups feared that the child exclusion provision would lead pregnant women to seek abortions, they insisted that the bonus be based on nonmarital births *and* abortions as a percentage of births to all women in the state, instead of just within the AFDC caseload, thus linking control of reproduction among AFDC women to control of all women in the state.

36. Center on Social Welfare Policy and Law, "State Welfare Reform Continues with Federal Waivers," *Welfare News*, 28 November 1994, pp. 9-10.

37. Timothy Egan, "Take This Bribe, Please, for Values to Be Received," *New York Times*, 12 November 1995, p. E5.

38. Moffitt, *Incentive Effects of the U.S. Welfare System;* U.S. Department of Health and Human Services, *Report to Congress on Out-Of-Wedlock Childbearing* (West Hyattsville, MD: Department of Health and Human Services, 1995, Exec. Summary, Monograph), pp. 2-3; House Committee on Ways and Means, *Overview of Entitlement Programs, 1994 Green Book*, p. 1111; Bureau of the Census, *Studies in Marriage and the Family, "Singleness in America," Current Population Reports*, Ser. P23, No. 162 (Washington, D.C.: Government Printing Office, 1990), p. 6.

39. House Committee on Ways and Means, *Overview of Entitlement Programs, 1994 Green Book*, p. 401; Government Accounting Office, *Families on Welfare: Teenage Mothers Least Likely to Become Self-Sufficient* (Washington, D.C.: Government Printing Office, 1994), pp. 16-17. In 1992 divorced women headed 37 percent of mother-only families, up somewhat from 32 percent in 1970. During the same period, however, the percentage of *never-married* single mothers surged from 7 percent to 36 percent of all single mothers.

40. Government Accounting Office, *Families on Welfare: Sharp Rise in Never-Married Women Reflects Societal Trends* (Washington, D.C.: Government Printing Office, 1994), pp. 16-17, 46-48; Bureau of the Census, *Martial Status and Living Arrangements, March 1993* (Washington, D.C.: Government Printing Office, 1994), p. xiii; House Committee on Ways and Means, *Overview of Entitlement Programs, 1994 Green Book*, p. 1111.

41. Mark Rank, "Fertility Among Women on Welfare: Incidence and Determinants," *American Sociological Review* 54 (April 1989): 296-304; House Committee on Ways and Means, *Overview of Entitlement Programs, 1994 Green Book*, p. 409.

42. Data from the 1988 National Survey of Family Growth indicate that 88 percent of the pregnancies experienced by never-married women, 69 percent of the pregnancies experienced by previously married women, and 40 percent of the pregnancies experienced by married women were unintended. U.S. Department of Health and Human Services, *Report to Congress on Out-Of-Wedlock Childbearing*, p. 8.

43. "Researchers Dispute Contention That Welfare Is a Major Cause of Out-of-Wedlock Births" (Press release issued by Sheldon Danziger, Director, Research and Training Programs on Poverty, the Underclass, and Public Policy, School of Social Work, University of Michigan, Ann Arbor, MI, 23 June 1994).

44. Center on Hunger, Poverty, and Nutrition Policy, "Statement on Key Welfare Reform Issues: The Empirical Evidence" (Medford, MA, 1995, Short brief), p. 3.

45. Government Accounting Office, *Families on Welfare: Teenage Mothers Least Likely To Become Self Sufficient*, p. 3; Department of Health and Human Services, *Report to Congress on Out-of-Wedlock Childbearing*, p. 2-4.

46. The Alan Gutmacher Institute reports that half the babies born to mothers aged fifteen to seventeen were fathered by men twenty years of age or older; 20 percent of the fathers were six or more years older than the teen mother. See Jennifer Steinhauer, "Study Cites Adult Males for Most Teen-Age Births," *New York Times*, 2 August 1995, p. A10.

47. Myron Magnet, "Problem No. 1: The Children," *New York Times*, 25 November 1994, p. A37.

48. Nina Bernstein, "Foster Care System Wary of Welfare Cuts," *New York Times*, 19 November 1995, pp. 1, 26.

49. David Lond, Robert Wood, and Hilary Kopp, "The Effects of LEAP and Enhanced Services in Cleveland, Ohio's, Learning, Earning, and Parenting Programs for Teenage Parents on Welfare" (New York: Manpower Demonstration Research Corporation, 1994, Report), p. vi.

50. Quoted in Ruth Coniff, "Big Bad Welfare," *The Progressive* (August 1994): 21; and Collins and Southwell, *Life on the Edge*, p. 11.

51. Lynn Woolsey, "Reinvent Welfare, Humanely," *New York Times*, 22 January 1994, p. 21.

52. Greg Duncan, Martha Hill, and Saul Hoffman, "Welfare Dependence Within and Across Generations," *Science* 239 (29 January 1988).

53. Levin-Epstein, "Rising Poverty Rates: Changes in Families and a Changing Economy," *Family Matters* 7, nos. 1-2 (Spring/Summer 1995): 3-4; "The Difference That Money Makes," pp. 9-10; "Researchers Dispute Contention That Welfare Is a Major Cause of Out-of-Wedlock Births" (Press release issued by Sheldon Danziger, Director, Research and Training Programs on Poverty, the Underclass, and Public Policy, School of Social Work, University of Michigan, Ann Arbor, MI, 23 June 1994).

54. Center on Budget and Policy Priorities, "Summary of Effects of House Bill H.R.4 on Low-Income Programs" (Washington, D.C., 16 May 1995, Short brief), p. 3.

55. Center on Social Welfare Policy and Law, "Summary of AFDC Waiver Activity Since February 1993" (Washington, D.C., April 1995, Short brief), pp. 2-3.

56. Bernstein, "Foster Care System Wary of Welfare Cuts," p. 26.

57. Center on Budget and Policy Priorities, "The New Fiscal Agenda: What Will It Mean and How Will It Be Accomplished?" (Washington, D.C., January 1995, Short brief).

58. Collins and Southwell, *Life on the Edge*, p. 2.

PART 2: A PROGRAM JUST FOR SINGLE MOTHERS

1. Stephanie Coontz, *The Social Origins of Private Life: A History of American Families, 1600-1900* (London: Verso, 1989), p. 167.

2. Mary Ryan, *Womanhood in America, from Colonial Times to the Present* (New York: New Viewpoints, 1975), pp. 100-101.

3. Benjamin Klebaner, "Poverty and Its Relief in American Thought, 1815-61," in *Compassion and Responsibility: Readings in the History of Social Welfare Policy in the United States*, ed. Frank R. Breul and Steven J. Diner (Chicago: University of Chicago Press, 1980), p. 123l.

4. Stephanie Coontz, *Social Origins of Private Life*, pp. 161-209.

5. Walter I. Trattner, *From Poor Law to Welfare State: A History of Social Welfare in America*, 4th ed. (New York: Free Press, 1989), p. 53.

6. Michael B. Katz, *In the Shadow of the Poorhouse: A Social History of Welfare in America* (New York: Basic Books, 1986), p. 23.

7. David Rothman, *The Discovery of Asylum: Social Order and Disorder in the New Republic* (Boston: Little, Brown and Co., 1971), p. 183; Walter I. Trattner, *From Poor Law to Welfare State*, pp. 55-56; Michael B. Katz, *In the Shadow of the Poorhouse*, pp. 37-42.

8. June Axinn and Herman Levin, *Social Welfare: A History of the American Response to Need* (New York: Harper and Row, 1975), p. 100.

9. Blanche Coll, *Perspectives in Public Welfare: A History* (Washington, D.C.: Department of Health, Education and Welfare, Office of Research, Demonstration and Training, 1969, Monograph), p. 43.

10. Michael B. Katz, *In the Shadow of the Poorhouse*, p. 37, Table 2.1.

11. Pricilla Ferguson Clement, "Nineteenth Century Welfare Policy, Programs and Poor Women: Philadelphia as a Case Study," *Feminist Studies* 1 (Spring 1992): 35-58 (p. 45, Table 5).

12. Blanche Coll, *Perspectives in Public Welfare*, p. 58.

13. David M. Schneider and Albert Deutch, *The History of Public Welfare in New York State, 1867-1940* (Chicago: University of Chicago Press, 1951), p. 38.

14. Joseph Rayback, *A History of American Labor* (New York: Free Press, 1960), p. 159.

15. David Gordon, Richard Edwards, and Michael Reich, *Segmented Work, Divided Workers: The Historical Transformation of Labor in the United States* (Cambridge and London: Cambridge University Press, 1982), pp. 56-100.

16. Christine Stansell, *City of Women: Sex and Class in New York 1789-1860* (Urbana: University of Illinois Press, 1987), pp. 63-75.

17. Michael B. Katz, *In the Shadow of the Poorhouse*, p. 108.

18. Lela Costin, "Cruelty to Children: A Dormant Issue and Rediscovery 1920-1960," *Social Service Review* 66, No. 2 (June 1992): 179.

19. Blanche Coll, *Perspectives in Public Welfare*, p. 68.

20. Unless otherwise indicated, the discussion of Mothers' Pensions draws on Mimi Abramovitz, *Regulating the Lives of Women: Social Welfare Policy from Colonial Times to the Present* (Boston: South End Press, 1988); Linda Gordon, *Pitied but Not Entitled: Single Mothers and the History of Welfare* (New York: Free Press, 1994); Mark H. Leff, "The Mothers' Pension Movement in the Progressive Era," in *Compassion and Responsibility*, ed. Frank R. Breul and Steven J. Diner, p. 247; and Gwendolyn Mink, *The Wages of Motherhood: Inequality in the Welfare State, 1917-1942* (Ithaca, NY: Cornell University Press, 1995).

21. Unless otherwise indicated, the discussion of ADC draws on Mimi Abramovitz, *Regulating the Lives of Women*; Eveline M. Burns, *The American Social Security System* (New York: Houghton Mifflin Co., 1949), p. 362; Linda Gordon, *Pitied but Not Entitled*; Gwendolyn Mink, *The Wages of*

Motherhood; and James Patterson, *America's Struggle Against Poverty 1900-1980* (Cambridge: Harvard University Press, 1981).

22. Jerry Cates, *Insuring Inequality: Administrative Leadership in Social Security, 1935-1954* (Ann Arbor, MI: University of Michigan Press, 1983).

23. Gwendolyn Mink, "Why Should Poor Single Mothers Have to Work Outside the Home?" (unpub. ms., 1995), p. 10.

24. U.S. Congress, Joint Economic Committee, Subcommittee on Fiscal Policy, *Studies in Public Welfare, Paper No. 20, Handbook of Public Income Transfer Programs, 1975* (Washington, D.C.: Government Printing Office, 1974), pp. 169-70, Tables 9 and 10.

25. James Patterson, *America's Struggle Against Poverty*, p. 78.

26. U.S. Congress, House Committee on Ways and Means, *Overview of Entitlement Programs, 1993 Green Book* (Washington, D.C.: Government Printing Office, 1993), p. 1313, Table 4.

27. Donald Bartlett and James B. Steele, *America: Who Really Pays the Taxes?* (New York: Simon and Schuster, 1994), pp. 68-69.

28. James Patterson, *America's Struggle Against Poverty*, pp. 89-90; Lucy Komisar, *Down and Out in the USA: A History of Social Welfare* (New York: New Viewpoints, 1974), pp. 72-73.

29. Susan Hartmann, *The Home Front and Beyond: American Women in the 1940s* (Boston: Twayne Publishers, 1982), p. 90.

30. Steven Mintz and Susan Kellog, *Domestic Revolutions: A Social History of American Family Life* (New York: Free Press, 1988), p. 161.

31. Alice Kessler-Harris, *Out to Work: A History of Wage Earning Women in the United States* (New York: Oxford University Press, 1982), p. 278.

32. Alice Kessler-Harris, *Out To Work*, p. 303.

33. Jacqueline Jones, *Labor of Love, Labor of Sorrow: Black Women, Work and the Family from Slavery to the Present* (New York: Basic Books, 1985), pp. 235, 258, 262.

34. Eveline M. Burns, *Social Security and Public Policy* (New York: McGraw Hill, 1956), p. 89.

35. The examples of AFDC restrictions are discussed in Linda Gordon, *Pitied but Not Entitled*, pp. 276, 414 (n. 103); Lucy Komisar, *Down and Out in the USA*, p. 83; Jacqueline Jones, *Labor of Love, Labor of Sorrow*, p. 26; Frances Fox Piven and Richard Cloward, *Regulating the Poor: The Functions of Public Welfare* (New York: Random House, 1993), pp. 128 (n. 3), 134.

36. Frances Fox Piven and Richard Cloward, *Regulating the Poor*, pp. 135, 136 (n. 17).

37. Susan M. Hartmann, *The Home Front and Beyond*, p. 165; Steven Mintz and Susan Kellog, *Domestic Revolutions*, pp. 170-72; Heather Ross and Isabel Sawhill, *Time of Transition: The Growth of Families Headed by Women* (Washington, D.C.: Urban Institute, 1975), p. 199, Table 1-M.

38. Linda Gordon, *Pitied but Not Entitled*, p. 35; Jacqueline Jones, *Labor of Love, Labor of Sorrow*, p. 263.

39. Steven Mintz and Susan Kellog, *Domestic Revolutions*, pp. 162-65; Mildred Rein, *Dilemmas of Welfare Policy: Why Work Strategies Haven't Worked* (New York: Praeger, 1982), pp. 15-16.

40. Eveline Burns, *Social Security and Public Policy*, p. 86, n. 13.

41. Daniel P. Moynihan, "Employment, Income and the Ordeal of the Negro

Family," *Daedalus: Journal of the American Academy of Arts and Sciences* 94, no. 4 (Fall 1965): 762-766; Michael K. Brown, "Divergent Fates: Race, Gender and the Legacy of the New Deal," (Conference Proceedings, Institute for Women's Policy Research, Washington, D.C., 1994)

42. James Patterson, *America's Struggle Against Poverty*, pp. 89-90.

43. The examples of AFDC rules and regulations are variously discussed in Linda Gordon "What Does Welfare Regulate?" *Social Research* 55, no. 4 (Winter 1988), p. 616; Komisar, *Down and Out in the USA*, pp. 79-80, 89; Patterson, *America's Struggle Against Poverty 1900-1980*, p. 88.

44. For examples of moral behavior standards detailed in the next two paragraphs see Komisar, *Down and Out in the USA*, p. 146; Piven and Cloward, *Regulating the Poor*, pp. 139-140, 169-170; Rickie Solinger, *Wake Up Little Susie: Single Pregnancy and Race Before Roe V. Wade* (New York: Routledge, 1992), pp. 51-56.

45. U.S. Congress, House Committee on Ways and Means, *Overview of Entitlement Programs, 1994 Green Book*, pp. 89, 395.

46. Frances Fox Piven and Richard Cloward, *Regulating the Poor*. This analysis has been challenged in Walter Trattner, ed., *Social Welfare or Social Control: Some Historical Reflections on Regulating the Poor* (Knoxville, TN: University of Tennessee Press, 1985), p. 36; and James Patterson, *America's Struggle Against Poverty*, p. 134.

47. The data in this paragraph can be found in James Patterson, *America's Struggle Against Poverty*, p. 172; Heather Ross and Isabel Sawhill, *Time of Transition*, p. 105; Gilbert Y. Steiner, *The State of Welfare* (Washington, D.C.: Brookings Institution, 1971), p. 41; U.S. Congress, Joint Economic Committee, Subcommittee on Fiscal Policy, *Studies in Public Welfare*, p. 169, Table 9.

48. Quoted in James Patterson, *America's Struggle Against Poverty*, pp. 172-73; Gilbert Y. Steiner, *The State of Welfare*, p. 49; and James Patterson, Ibid., pp. 89-90.

49. Heather Ross and Isabel Sawhill, *Time of Transition*, p. 98; Mildred Rein, *Dilemmas of Welfare Policy: Why Work Strategies Haven't Worked* (New York: Praeger, 1982), pp. 8-9; Sar Levitan, Martin Rein, and David Marwick, *Work and Welfare Go Together* (Baltimore: Johns Hopkins Press, 1972), p. 14; Steiner, *The State of Welfare*, p. 41; and U.S. Congress, Joint Economic Committee, *Income Security For Americans: Recommendations of the Public Welfare Study* (Washington, D.C.: Government Printing Office, 1974), p. 72.

50. The discussion of WIN draws on Sar Levitan, Martin Rein, and David Marwick, *Work and Welfare Go Together*; Mildred Rein, *Dimensions of Welfare Policy*; Nancy Rose, *Workfare or Fair Work: Women, Welfare, and Government Work Programs* (New Brunswick, NJ: Rutgers University Press, 1995), chap. 6; U.S. Congress, Joint Economic Committee, *Income Security for Americans: Recommendations of the Public Welfare Study* (Washington, D.C.: Government Printing Office; General Accounting Office, 1974); and Comptroller General of the United States, *An Overview of the WIN Program: Its Objectives, Accomplishments and Problems* (Washington, D.C.: Government Printing Office, 1982).

51. For the data on the marital status of AFDC mothers during this period see Joel Handler and Yeheskel Hasenfeld, *The Moral Construction of Poverty* (Newbury Park: Sage Publications, 1991), p. 114; Gilbert Y. Steiner, *The State of Welfare*, p.42; and U.S. Congress, House Committee on Ways and Means, *Overview of Entitlement Programs, 1993 Green Book*, p. 696, Table 31.

52. Johnnie Tillmon, "Welfare Is a Women's Issue," *Liberation News Service*, no. 415 (26 February 1972), reprinted in *American Working Women: A Documentary History 1600 to the Present*, ed. Rosalyn Baxandall, Linda Gordon, and Susan Reverby (New York: Vintage Books, 1976), pp. 354-58.
53. Lucy Komisar, *Down and Out in the USA*, p. 146.
54. Rickie Solinger, *Wake Up Little Susie*, p. 49, citing Julius Horowitz, "The Arithmetic of Delinquency," *New York Times Magazine*, 31 January 1965, p. 12.
55. Daniel P. Moynihan, "The Negro Family: The Case For National Action," in *The Moynihan Report and the Politics of Controversy*, ed. L. Rainwater and W. Yancy (Cambridge: MIT Press, 1967), pp. 39-125.

PART 3: THE GENDERED WELFARE STATE

1. The following definitions of patriarchy draw on Michelle Barrett, *Women's Oppression Today* (London: Verso, 1980); Martha Albertson Fineman, *The Neutered Mother, The Sexual Family, and Other Twentieth-Century Tragedies* (New York: Routledge, 1995); Iris Young, "Is Male Gender Identity the Cause of Male Domination?" in *Mothering Essays in Feminist Theory*, ed. Joyce Trebilcot (Totowa, NJ: Rowman and Allenheld, 1984), pp. 129-46; Gerda Lerner, *The Creation of Patriarchy* (New York: Oxford University Press, 1986); Sylvia Walby, *Patriarchy at Work* (Minneapolis: University of Minnesota Press, 1986).
2. Mimi Abramovitz, *Regulating the Lives of Women: Social Welfare Policy from Colonial Times to the Present* (Boston, MA: South End Press, 1988).
3. Evelyn Nakamo Glenn, "Racial Ethnic Women's Labor: The Intersection of Race, Gender, and Class Oppression," *Review of Radical Political Economics* 17, no. 3 (1985): 86-108.
4. See Johanna Brenner and Barbara Laslett, "Social Reproduction and the Family," in *The Social Reproduction of Organization and Culture*, ed. Ulf Himmelstrand (London: Sage Publications, 1986), pp. 115-31; Renate Bridenthal, "The Dialectics of Production and Reproduction in History," *Radical America* 10, no. 2 (March/April 1976): 3-11; Barbara Laslett, "Production, Reproduction and Social Change," in *The State of Sociology: Problems and Prospects*, ed. James F. Short, Jr. (Beverly Hills, CA: Sage, 1981), pp. 239-58; Natalie J. Sokoloff, *Between Money and Love: The Dialectics of Women's Home and Market Work* (New York: Praeger, 1981); Lise Vogel, *Marxism and the Oppression of Women: Toward a Unitary Theory* (New Brunswick, NJ: Rutgers University Press, 1983).
5. See for example, Richard Titmuss, *Essays on the Welfare State* (London: Allen and Unwin, 1958); Harold Wilensky and Charles Lebaux, *Industrial Society and Social Welfare* (New York: Russell Sage, 1958); Harold Wilensky, *The Welfare State and Equality* (Berkeley: University of California Press, 1975).
6. T. H. Marshall, *Citizenship and Social Class* (Cambridge: Cambridge University Press, 1950); Ramish Mishra, *Society and Social Policy: Theories and Practice of Welfare* (London: Macmillan, 1981).
7. Ian Gough, *The Political Economy of Welfare* (London: Macmillan, 1979); James O'Connor, *The Fiscal Crisis of the State* (New York: St. Martin's Press, 1973); Mishra, *Society and Social Policy*, 68-96.

8. Some of the most important of these works are, in alphabetical order: Abramovitz, *Regulating the Lives of Women;* Margaret Benston, "The Political Economy of Women's Liberation," *Monthly Review* 21, no. 4 (September 1969): 13-27; Johanna Brenner and Barbara Laslett, "Gender, Social Reproduction, and Women's Self-Organization: Considering the U.S. Welfare State," *Gender and Society* 5, no. 3 (September 1991): 311-33; Brenner and Laslett, "Social Reproduction and the Family," pp. 115-31; Carol Brown, "Mothers, Fathers and Children: From Private to Public Patriarchy," in *Women and Revolution,* ed. Lydia Sargent (Boston: South End Press, 1981); Stephanie Coontz, *The Social Origins of Private Life: A History of American Families 1600-1900* (London: Verso, 1988); Maria Della Costa, *The Power of Women and the Subversion of the Community* (Bristol: Falling Wall Press, 1973), pp. 19-54; Zillah Eisenstein, *Feminism and Sexual Equality: Crisis in Liberal America* (New York: Monthly Review Press, 1984); Betty Friedan, *The Feminine Mystique* (New York: Dell, 1963); Maxine Fuller, "Sex Role Stereotyping and Social Science," in *The Sex Role System: Psychological and Sociological Perspectives,* ed. J. Chetwynd and D. Hartness (Boston: Routledge and Kegan Paul, 1978); Linda Gordon, *Pitied But Not Entitled: Single Mothers and the History of Welfare* (New York: Free Press, 1994); Linda Gordon, ed., *Women, the State and Welfare* (Madison, WI: University of Wisconsin Press, 1990); Heidi Hartmann, "The Family as the Locus of Gender, Class, and Political Struggle: The Example of Housework," *Signs* 6 (Spring 1981): 366-94; Barbara Hobson, "Economic Dependency and Women's Social Citizenship: Some Thoughts on Epsing-Anderson's Welfare State Regimes" (Paper presented at the Conference on Gender, Citizenship and Social Policy, 31 October 1991); Laslett, "Production, Reproduction and Social Change," pp. 239-58; Mary McIntosh, "The State and the Oppression of Women," in *Feminism and Materialism,* ed. Annette Kuhn and Anne Wolpe (London: Routledge and Kegan Paul, 1978), pp. 254-89; Steven Mintz and Susan Kellog, *Domestic Revolutions: A Social History of American Family Life* (New York: Free Press, 1988); Robyn Muncy, *Creating a Female Dominion in American Reform, 1890-1935* (New York: Oxford University Press, 1991), chaps. 2 and 3; Mary O'Brien, *The Politics of Reproduction* (London: Routledge and Kegan Paul, 1981); Ann S. Orloff, "Gender and the Social Rights of Citizenship: The Comparative Analysis of Gender Relations and Welfare States," *American Sociological Review* 58, no. 3 (June 1993): 303-28; Theda Skocpol, *Protecting Soldiers and Mothers: The Political Origins of Social Policy in the United States* (Cambridge, MA: Harvard University Press, 1992); Karen Skold, "The Interests of Feminists and Children in Child Care" in *Feminism, Children, and the New Families,* ed. S.M. Dornbusch & M. H. Strober (New York: Guilford Press, 1988), pp. 113-36; Sokoloff, *Between Money and Love;* Barbara Thorne, "Feminist Rethinking of the Family: An Overview," in *Rethinking the Family: Some Feminist Questions,* ed. Barbara Thorne and Marilyn Yalom (New York: Longman, 1982), pp. 1-24; Vogel, *Marxism and the Oppression of Women;* Susan Ware, *Beyond Suffrage: Women in the New Deal* (Cambridge, MA: Harvard University Press, 1981); Batya Weinbaum and Amy Bridges, "The Other Side of the Paycheck: Monopoly Capital and the Structure of Consumption," *Monthly Review* 28

(July/August 1976): 88-103; Elizabeth Wilson, *Women and the Welfare State* (London: Tavistock, 1977); Maxine Baca Zinn, "Family, Feminism and Race in America," *Gender & Society* 4, no. 1 (March 1990): 68-82; Eli Zaretsky, "The Place of the Family in the Origins of the Welfare State," in *Rethinking the Family,* ed. Thorne and Yalom, pp. 1-24.

9. Abramovitz, *Regulating the Lives of Women;* McIntosh, "The State and the Oppression of Women," pp. 254-89; O'Brien, *The Politics of Reproduction;* Wilson, *Women and the Welfare State;* Virginia Sapiro, "The Gender Basis of American Social Policy," in *Women, the State, and Welfare,* ed. Gordon, pp. 36-55.

10. Hobson, "Economic Dependency and Women's Social Citizenship"; Hartmann, "The Family as the Locus of Gender, Class, and Political Struggle," pp. 366-94; Coontz, *The Social Origins of Private Life;* Susan Schecter, *Women and Male Violence* (Boston, MA: South End Press, 1982); Linda Gordon, "Family Violence, Feminism, and Social Control," in Gordon, *Women, the State and Welfare,* pp. 178-99; Orloff, "Gender and the Social Rights of Citizenship," pp. 303-28.

11. Patricia Ann Collins, *Black Feminist Thought: Knowledege, Consciousness and the Politics of Empowerment* (New York: Harper Collins, 1990), pp. 43-66; Glenn, "Racial Ethnic Women's Labor," pp. 86-108; Zinn, "Family, Feminism and Race in America," pp. 68-82.

12. Linda Gordon, "The New Feminist Scholarship on the Welfare State," in *Women, the State, and Welfare,* ed. Gordon, pp. 9-35; Barbara Nelson, "The Origins of the Two-Channel Welfare State: Workmen's Compensation and Mother's Aid," in *Women, the State and Welfare,* ed. Gordon, pp. 123-51; Sapiro, "The Gender Basis of American Social Policy," pp. 36-55.

13. See, for example, Nancy Fraser and Linda Gordon, "Contract Versus Charity: Why There Is No Social Citizenship in the United States," *Socialist Review* 22, no. 3 (July/August 1992): 45-67; Orloff, "Gender and the Social Rights of Citizenship," pp. 303-28; Orloff, "Gender and the Welfare State," *American Review of Sociology* 22 (1996); Carole Pateman, "The Patriarchal Welfare State," in *Democracy and the Welfare State,* ed. Amy Gutmann (Princeton, NJ: Princeton University Press, 1988), pp. 231-60.

14. For a discussion of this, see Zillah Eisenstein, "Constructing a Theory of Capitalist Patriarchy and Socialist Feminism," in *Women, Class and the Feminist Imagination,* ed. K. Hansen and I. Philipson (Philadelphia, PA: Temple University Press, 1990), pp. 114-45; Vogel, *Marxism and the Oppression of Women.*

15. Gough, *The Political Economy of Welfare;* O'Connor, *The Fiscal Crisis of the State.*

16. Gordon, *Pitied But Not Entitled;* Gwendolyn Mink, *The Wages of Motherhood: Inequality in the Welfare State, 1917-1942* (Ithaca, NY: Cornell University Press, 1995), p. 1.

17. Hartmann, "The Unhappy Marriage of Marxism and Feminism," pp. 1-43; Eisenstein, *Feminism and Sexual Equality;* Sokoloff, *Between Money and Love;* Walby, *Patriarchy at Work;* McIntosh, "The State and the Oppression of Women," pp. 253-89; Pateman, "The Patriarchal Welfare State," pp. 231-60; Frances Fox Piven, "Women, the State and Ideology," in *Gender and the Life Course,* ed. Alice Rossi (New York: Aldine, 1985).

18. See Abramovitz, *Regulating the Lives of Women,* pp. 254-60; Jane Ross and

Melinda Opp, "Treatment of Women In the U.S. Social Security System," *Social Security Bulletin* 53, no. 3 (1993): 56-67; Maxine Ferber, "Women's Employment and the Social Security System," *Social Security Bulletin* 56, no. 3 (1993): 43-55.

19. Brenner and Laslett, "Social Reproduction and the Family," pp. 120-21; Bridenthal, "The Dialectics of Production and Reproduction in History," pp. 3-11; Carol Ehrlich, "The Unhappy Marriage of Marxism and Feminism: Can It Be Saved?" in *Women and Revolution: A Discussion of the Unhappy Marriage of Marxism and Feminism,* ed. Lydia Sargent (Boston, MA: South End Press, 1981), pp. 109-35; McIntosh, "The State and the Oppression of Women," pp. 254-89; O'Brien, *The Politics of Reproduction;* Sokoloff, *Between Money and Love;* Young, "Beyond the Unhappy Marriage: A Critique of the Dual Systems Theory," pp. 43-71.

20. Zillah Eisenstein, *The Radical Future of Liberal Feminism* (New York: Longman, 1981).

21. Orloff, "Gender and the Social Rights of Citizenship," pp. 303-28; Nancy Fraser, "After the Family Wage: What Do Women Want In Social Welfare," in "Women and Welfare Reform: A Policy Conference" (Proceedings of conference sponsored by the Institute For Women's Policy Research, Washington, D.C., 23 October 1993).

22. Pateman, "The Patriarchal Welfare State," pp. 231-60.

PART 4: FIGHTING BACK: FROM THE LEGISLATURE TO THE ACADEMY TO THE STREETS

1. Guida West and Rhoda Lois Blumberg, *Women and Social Protest* (New York: Oxford University Press, 1990), p. 7.

2. See Walter Korpi, *The Working Class and Welfare Capitalism: Work, Unions and Politics in Sweden* (London: Routledge & Kegan Paul, 1978), chap. 1; Ramesh Mishra, *Society and Social Policy: Theories and Practice of Welfare,* 2nd ed. (London: Macmillan, 1981), chaps. 1 and 2.

3. Gosta Epsing-Anderson, *Three Worlds of Welfare Capitalism* (Princeton, NJ: Princeton University Press, 1990); Gosta Epsing-Anderson, *Politics Against Markets: The Social Democratic Road to Power* (Princeton, NJ: Princeton University Press, 1985); Korpi, *The Working Class and Welfare Capitalism.*

4. Korpi, *The Working Class and Welfare Capitalism,* pp. 5-10; Mishra, *Society and Social Policy,* pp. 68-87; Paul M. Sweezy, *The Theory of Capitalist Development* (New York: Monthly Review Press, 1968), pp. 244-50.

5. Diane Balser, *Sisterhood and Solidarity: Feminism and Labor in Modern Times* (Boston, MA: South End Press, 1987); Philip Foner, *Women and the American Labor Movement from World War I to the Present* (New York: Free Press, 1980); Barbara Kingsolver, *Women in the Great Arizona Mine Strike of 1983* (Ithaca, NY: ILR Press, 1989); Ruth Milkman, ed., *Women, Work, and Protest: A Century of U.S. Women's Labor History (Boston, MA: Routledge & Kegan Paul, 1985).*

6. Ann Bookman and Sandra Morgen, eds., *Women and the Politics of Empowerment* (Philadelphia, PA: Temple University Press, 1988); Nancy Hewitt and Suzanne Lebsock, *Visible Women: New Essays on American Activism* (Urbana,

IL: University of Illinois Press, 1991); Ida Susser, *Norman Street: Poverty and Politics In an Urban Neighborhood* (New York: Oxford University Press, 1982); Ann Gibson Robinson, *The Montgomery Bus Boycott and the Women Who Started It* (Knoxville: University of Tennessee Press, 1987); Nancy Naples, "Contradictions in the Gender Subtext of the War on Poverty: The Community Work and Resistance of Women from Low-Income Communities," *Social Problems* 38, no. 3 (1991): 316-32.

7. Linda Gordon, *Heroes of Their Own Lives: The Politics and History of Family Violence* (New York: Penguin Books, 1988); Susan Handley Hertz, *The Welfare Mothers Movement: A Decade of Change for Poor Women* (Washington, D.C.: University Press of America, 1981); Megan H. Morrissey, "The Downtown Welfare Advocate Center: A Case Study of a Welfare Rights Organization," *Social Service Review* 64, no. 2 (June 1990): 189-20; Frances Fox Piven and Richard A. Cloward, *Poor People's Movements: Why They Succeed, How They Fail* (New York: Vintage Books, 1979), pp. 264-362; Jackie Pope, "Women in the Welfare Rights Struggle: The Brooklyn Welfare Action Council," in *Women and Social Protest*, ed. West and Blumberg, pp. 57-74; Guida West, *The National Welfare Rights Movement: The Social Protest of Poor Women* (New York: Praeger, 1981).

8. Kathleen Blee, "Family Patterns and the Politicization of Consumption Relations," *Sociological Spectrum* 5, no. 4 (1985): 295-316; Dana Frank, "Housewives, Socialists, and the Politics of Food: The 1917 Cost-of-Living Protests," *Feminist Studies* 11, no. 2 (1985): 265-85; Paula Hyman, "Immigrant Women and Consumer Protest: The New York City Kosher Meat Boycott of 1902," *American Jewish History* 70 (Summer 1980): 91-105; Tamar Kaplan, "Female Consciousness and Collective Action: Barcelona, 1910-1918," *Signs* 7 (1982): 545-65; Barbara Laslett and Johanna Brenner, "Gender and Social Reproduction: Historical Perspectives," *Annual Review of Sociology* 15 (1989):381-404; Batya Weinbaum and Amy Bridges, "The Other Side of the Paycheck: Monopoly Capital and the Structure of Consumption," in *Capitalist Patriarchy and the Case For Socialist Feminism*, ed. Zillah Eisenstein (New York: Monthly Review Press, 1979), pp. 90-205.

9. George Rudé, *The Crowd in History* (New York: Wiley, 1964).

10. The discussion of nineteenth-century reform draws on: Eleanor Flexner, *Century of Struggle: The Women' s Rights Movement in the United States* (New York: Atheneum, 1968); Nancy E. McGlen and Karen O'Conner, *Women's Rights: The Struggle for Equality in the Nineteenth and Twentieth Centuries* (New York: Praeger, 1983); Mary Ryan, *Womanhood in America: From Colonial Times to the Present* (New York: New Viewpoints, 1975), pp. 137-92; Theda Skocpol, *Protecting Soldiers and Mothers: The Political Origins of Social Policy in the United States* (Cambridge, MA: Harvard University Press, 1992).

11. The discussion of Progressive Era and New Deal activism by white women draws on: Johanna Brenner and Barbara Laslett, "Gender, Social Reproduction, and Women's Self-Organization: Considering the U.S. Welfare State," *Gender and Society* 5, no. 3 (September 1991): 311-33; Linda Gordon, *Pitied But Not Entitled: Single Mothers and the History of Welfare* (New York: Free Press, 1994); Robyn Muncy, *Creating a Female Dominion in American Reform, 1890-1935* (New York: Oxford University Press, 1991), chaps. 2 and 3; Skoc-

pol, *Protecting Soldiers and Mothers;* Susan Ware, *Beyond Suffrage: Women in the New Deal* (Cambridge, MA: Harvard University Press, 1981).

12. The phenomenon of female social reform was not unique to the United States. During the same period, intense activism by European women helped to forge the modern welfare state in France and Britain. See Beth Koven and Sonya Michel, "Womanly Duties: Maternalist Politics and the Origins of Welfare States in France, Germany, Great Britain, and the United States" (unpub. ms., 19 October 1990).

13. The debate about whether social policy that treats women as equals of men is better for women than social policy that treats women and men differently based on their unique differences has continued to rage.

14. The discussion of Progressive Era and New Deal activism among African-American women draws on: Eileen Boris, "The Power of Motherhood: Black and White Activist Women Redefine the Political," in *Mothers of a New World: Maternalist Politics and the Origins of the Welfare State,* ed. Beth Koven and Sonya Michel (New York: Routledge, 1993), pp. 213-46; Angela Davis, *Women, Race, and Class* (New York: Vintage, 1983); Paula Giddings, *When and Where I Enter: The Impact of Black Women on Race and Sex in America* (Toronto: Bantam Books, 1984); Gordon, *Pitied But Not Entitled,* chap. 5; Darlene Clark Hine, "Lifting the Veil, Shattering the Silence: Black Women's History in Slavery and Freedom," in *The State of Afro-American History, Past, Present and Future,* ed. D. C. Hine (Baton Rouge: Louisiana State University Press, 1986), pp. 223-52; Gerda Lerner, *Black Women in White America: A Documentary History* (New York: Vintage Books, 1973); Gwendolyn Mink, *The Wages of Motherhood: Inequality in the Welfare State, 1917-1942* (Ithaca, NY: Cornell University Press, 1995); Ann Firor Scott, "On Seeing and Not Seeing: A Case of Historical Invisibility," *Journal of American History* 7 (June 1984): 7-21; Deborah Gray White, "The Cost of Club Work, the Price of Black Feminism," in *Visible Women: New Essays On American Activism* (Urbana: University of Illinois Press, 1993), pp. 247-69.

15. Laslett and Brenner, "Gender and Social Reproduction," pp. 381-404

16. Gordon, *Pitied But Not Entitled;* Alice Kessler Harris, "Women and Welfare: Public Interventions in Private Lives," *Radical History Review* 56 (1993): 127-36.

17. Dorothy Gallagher, review of *Florence Kelly and the Nation's Work* by Kathryn Kish Sklar, *New York Times Book Review,* 9 July 1995, p. 9.

18. Gordon, *Pitied But Not Entitled,* pp. 55-56; Koven and Michel, "Womanly Duties"; Aileen Kraditor, *Ideas of the Women's Suffrage Movement, 1880-1920* (New York: W. W. Norton, 1981), p. 67; Muncy, *Creating a Female Dominion in American Reform.*

19. Dana Frank, "Food Wins All Struggles: Seattle Labor and the Politicization of Consumption," *Radical History Review* 51 (1991): 65-89.

20. For a detailed discussion of these events, see Frank, "Housewives, Socialists, and the Politics of Food," pp. 265-85; William Frieburger, "War, Prosperity, and Hunger: The New York Food Riots," *Labor History* 25 (Spring 1984): 217-39; Hyman, "Immigrant Women and Consumer Protest," pp. 91-105; Annelise Orleck, "Common Sense and a Little Fire: Working-Class Women's Activism in the Twentieth Century United States" (Ph.D. diss., New York University, 1989), pp. 540-42; Judith Smith,

"Our Own Kind: Family and Networks in Providence," in *A Heritage of Her Own: Toward a New Social History of American Women*, ed. Nancy Cott and Elizabeth H. Pleck (New York: Simon and Schuster, 1979), pp. 393-411.

21. Lerner, *Black Women in White America*, pp. 211-12.

22. John Ehrenreich, *The Altruistic Imagination: A History of Social Work and Social Policy in the United States* (Ithaca, NY: Cornell University Press, 1985), p. 49; William Graebner, *The Engineering of Consent: Democracy and Authority in Twentieth-Century America* (Madison, WI: University of Wisconsin Press, 1987), pp. 58-59.

23. Ruth Schwartz Cowan, "Two Washes in the Morning and a Bridge Party at Night: The American Housewife Between the Wars," *Women's Studies* 3 (1976): 147-72; Heidi Hartmann, "Capitalism and Women's Work in the Home, 1900-1950" (Ph.D. diss., Yale University, 1984), pp. 68-69.

24. Orleck, *Common Sense and a Little Fire*, pp. 556-58.

25. Unless otherwise noted, the discussion of the community-based cost of living protests during the 1920s, 1930s, and 1940s draws on Orleck, *Common Sense and a Little Fire*, chap. 8, "We Are That Mythic Thing Called the Public—Militant Housewives During the Great Depression," pp. 534-609.

26. Anne Stein, "Postwar Consumer Boycotts," *Radical America* 9 (July-August 1975): 156-61.

27. The discussion of these groups is based largely on Verta Taylor, "Social Movement Continuity: The Women's Movement in Abeyance," *American Sociological Review* 54, no. 5 (October 1989): 761-76; Leila Rupp and Verta Taylor, *Survival in the Doldrums: The American Women's Rights Movement, 1945 to the 1960s* (New York: Oxford University Press, 1987).

28. Jo Ann Gibson Robinson, *The Montgomery Bus Boycott and the Women Who Started It* (Knoxville: University of Tennessee Press, 1987); Janelle Scott, "Local Leadership in the Woman Suffrage Movement: Houston's Campaign for the Vote, 1917-1918," *Houston Review* 12, no. 1 (1990): 3-22.

29. For example, the NAACP leadership included Ruby Hurley (youth director), Daisy Bates (president, Little Rock, Arkansas, chapter), Rosa Parks (secretary, Montgomery, Alabama, chapter), and Ella Baker (president, New York City chapter and national director of branch work). Women were also active in the Urban League (formed in 1911); the Congress of Racial Equality (1943); the National Negro Labor Council (1951); the Southern Christian Leadership Conference (1957); and the Student Non-Violent Coordinating Committee (1960).

30. Giddings, *When and Where I Enter*, pp. 291-92.

31. Shulamit Reinharz, "Women as Competent Community Builders: The Other Side of the Coin," in *Social and Psychological Problems of Women: Prevention and Crisis*, ed. Annette U. Rickel, Meg Gerrard and Ira Iscoe (Washington, D.C.: Hemisphere Publishing Corporation, 1984), pp. 19-43; Jacqueline Jones, *Labor of Love, Labor of Sorrow: Black Women, Work, and the Family from Slavery to the Present* (New York: Basic Books, 1985), pp. 310-21.

32. Susan Lynn, *Progressive Women in Conservative Times: Racial Justice, Peace, and Feminism, 1945-1960* (New Brunswick, NJ: Rutgers University Press, 1992); Myra Marx Ferree and Beth B. Hess, *Controversy and Coalition: The New Feminist Movement* (Boston, MA: Twayne Publishers, 1985).

33. William Henry Chafe, *The American Woman: Her Changing Social, Economic and Political Roles, 1920-1970* (London: Oxford University Press, 1974); Sara Evans, *Born for Liberty: A History of Women in America* (New York: Free Press, 1989).

34. The discussion of welfare rights before the formation of the National Welfare Rights Organization relies on Hertz, *The Welfare Mothers' Movement;* Morrissey, "The Downtown Welfare Advocate Center," pp. 189-207; Piven and Cloward, *Poor People's Movements*, pp. 264-362; Pope, "Women in the Welfare Rights Struggle," pp. 57-74.

35. Unless otherwise noted, this discussion of the National Welfare Rights Organization relies on Martha Davis, "Welfare Rights and Women's Rights in the 1960s" (Paper presented at the Integrating the Sixties Conference, Washington, D.C., 30 May 1995); Piven and Cloward, *Poor People's Movements*, pp. 264-362; West, *The National Welfare Rights Movement*.

36. The percent of white women on welfare rose from 46.9 percent in 1973 to 50.2 percent in 1977, while the percent of black women fell off. See West, *The National Welfare Rights Movement*, p. 262.

37. Davis, "Welfare Rights and Women's Rights in the 1960s," pp. 21-22.

38. Testimony of Marian Kramer, president, National Welfare Rights Union, before the Subcommittee on Human Resources, Government Operations Committee, Washington, D.C., 10 March 1994, p. 1.

39. Up and Out of Poverty, Now! Coalition, The Grassroots Organizing Campaign to Redefine Welfare Reform, Grant Proposal, October 1994.

40. Nina Schuyler, "Under Attack but Fighting Back: The Birth of the Poor Women's Movement," *On the Issues* (Winter 1992): 22-28.

41. Johnnie Tillmon, "Welfare Is a Women's Issue," in *American Working Women: A Documentary History from 1600 to the Present*, ed. Rosalyn Baxandall, Linda Gordon, and Susan Reverby (New York: Vintage Books, 1976), p. 358.

42. *Survival News* (Fall/Winter 1994): 29.

43. AARP Women's Initiative Network, *Newsletter*, Spring 1995.

44. Barbara Bergman and Heidi Hartmann, "A Welfare Reform Based on Help for Working Parents," *Feminist Economics* 1, no. 2 (1995): 85-89.

45. Nancy Fraser, "After the Family Wage: What Do Women Want in Social Welfare?" in "Women and Welfare Reform: A Policy Conference" (Proceedings of conference sponsored by the Institute for Women's Policy Research, Washington, D.C., 23 October 1993).

46. Ann S. Orloff, "Gender and the Social Rights of Citizenship: A Comparative Analysis of Gender Relations and Welfare States," *American Sociological Review* 58, no. 3 (June 1993): pp. 303-28.

47. Martha Albertson Fineman, *The Neutered Mother, the Sexual Family, and Other Twentieth-Century Tragedies* (New York: Routledge, 1995).

48. Testimony of Marian Kramer, before the Subcommittee on Human Resources, p. 2.

49. Nancy Fraser, "After the Family Wage."

INDEX

 Home Sweet Forever Home

Don't miss the other
Invincible Girls Club adventures!

Art with Heart

THE INVINCIBLE GIRLS CLUB

BOOK 1

HOME SWEET FOREVER HOME

by Rachele Alpine

illustrated by Addy Rivera Sonda

Aladdin

New York   London   Toronto   Sydney   New Delhi

ALADDIN

An imprint of Simon & Schuster Children's Publishing Division

1230 Avenue of the Americas, New York, New York 10020

First Aladdin paperback edition May 2021

Text copyright © 2021 by Rachele Alpine

Illustrations copyright © 2021 by Addy Rivera Sonda

Also available in an Aladdin hardcover edition.

All rights reserved, including the right of reproduction in whole or in part in any form.

ALADDIN and related logo are registered trademarks of Simon & Schuster, Inc.

For information about special discounts for bulk purchases, please contact

Simon & Schuster Special Sales at 1-866-506-1949 or business@simonandschuster.com.

The Simon & Schuster Speakers Bureau can bring authors to your live event. For more information or to book an event contact the Simon & Schuster Speakers Bureau at 1-866-248-3049 or visit our website at www.simonspeakers.com.

Book designed by Heather Palisi

The illustrations for this book were rendered digitally.

The text of this book was set in Celeste.

Manufactured in the United States of America 0321 OFF

2 4 6 8 10 9 7 5 3 1

Library of Congress Cataloging-in-Publication Data

Names: Alpine, Rachele, 1979- author. | Sonda, Addy Rivera, illustrator.

Title: Home sweet forever home / by Rachele Alpine ; illustrated by Addy Rivera Sonda.

Description: First Aladdin paperback edition. | New York : Aladdin, 2021. |

Series: The invincible girls club; book 1 | Audience: Ages 7 to 10. | Audience: Grades 2–5. |

Summary: While volunteering at an animal shelter, Lauren and her three best friends—Ruby, Myka, and Emelyn—plan a cupcake adoption event to help older dogs find a home, but the big day does not go as planned.

Identifiers: LCCN 2020031906 (print) | LCCN 2020031907 (ebook) |

ISBN 9781534475304 (hardcover) | ISBN 9781534475298 (paperback) |

ISBN 9781534475311 (ebook)

Subjects: CYAC: Dogs—Fiction. | Animal shelters—Fiction. | Best friends—Fiction. | Friendship—Fiction.

Classification: LCC PZ7.A46255 Ho 2021 (print) | LCC PZ7.A46255 (ebook) | DDC [Fic]—dc23

LC record available at https://lccn.loc.gov/2020031906

LC ebook record available at https://lccn.loc.gov/2020031907

To Harrison . . .
When you smile, I am undone.

Do the thing you think you cannot do.
-Eleanor Roosevelt

Contents

THE ULTI-MUTT DAY

Today was the big day.

The day I had waited for my entire life.

I could hardly believe it, but I, Lauren Ellen Connors, was headed to the dog shelter.

Yep, that's right. I was Erie County Animal Shelter's newest volunteer!

This was a very big deal. I loved dogs. In fact, if there's something greater than love, that's what I felt toward dogs.

Unfortunately, I couldn't *have* a dog because my stepdad, Scott, was allergic to them.

Actually, "allergic" wasn't a strong enough word to describe what happened when he was around dogs or cats. His eyes became red and itchy, his face swelled up and got puffy, and he'd sneeze a million times. I felt bad for him, really I did, but I was also super bummed that I'd never know how awesome it was to grow up with a dog. Sure, Mom and Scott had tried to make up for it by letting me have the non-furry kinds of pets. I'd had three fish, a turtle, and a hermit crab, but it wasn't the same. You can't take a fish on a walk. A turtle will never play catch. And forget trying to snuggle up with a hermit crab. They pinch!

"I'm doomed to a childhood without a dog, and I always thought that was the most heartbreaking story ever told," I said to Mom as we drove to the shelter. "But now there's a happy ending!"

Once a week I was going to volunteer around the shelter, and then, the best part . . . I got to read to the dogs! The shelter had a program called Paws for Reading, which helped the dogs get used to people so that the dogs could find a forever home. Reading to them was a big responsibility. I had an important job to do.

I played with the zipper on my backpack. While I was about to burst from excitement, I had to admit that I was also nervous. Would the dogs like me? Would I do a good enough job? What if I messed up and the shelter never wanted me back?

Mom caught my eye in the rearview mirror, and it was as if she'd read my mind. "Relax, sweetie. The dogs will love you."

"Are you sure?"

"Without a doubt. How could they resist you?"

Mom's words made me feel a bit better, and the bubbly nervous feeling inside calmed down as she turned into the shelter's parking lot. I leaned forward to get a better look, but was hugely disappointed.

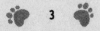

The shelter wasn't anything special at all.

It was a normal boring concrete building with a few windows on the front and a chain-link fence. There was a small parking lot and a few signs letting everyone know it was the animal shelter. You'd think that a place that housed such awesomeness would be more spectacular. I'm talking a spotlight, glitter cannon, and fireworks.

Oh well. People always say you can't judge a book by its cover and it's what's inside that counts.

And what could be better than a building full of dogs?

Um, nothing!

I jumped out of the car after Mom turned off the engine, and I spread my arms wide.

"Hello, doggies! I can't wait to meet you!" I shouted to the building.

I heard someone giggle, and I spotted two of my best friends, Ruby and Emelyn, waiting for me on a bench.

"Your big day has arrived!" Ruby announced. My friends were well aware of my dog obsession.

"I'm so glad you're here," I said, and gave each of them a giant hug. Reading to the dogs was going to be awesome, but reading to them with my best friends—Ruby, Emelyn, and Myka—was going to be stupendous. It had been a no-brainer to invite them. The four of us had been inseparable since our parents had met at the library's story time when we were babies. Well, everyone except Myka. Her mom was in the military, so they moved a lot. We lucked out last year when they moved to our town. Myka instantly fit into our group, and it was like we had all been friends forever.

"Are you kidding me? We wouldn't have missed this for anything." Ruby held up her grandma's old phone that she always had with her. She couldn't call or text anyone with it but was constantly taking pictures or videos and using the notes app to write down any good scoops she stumbled upon. She wanted to be a world-famous journalist and wasn't shy about asking people questions. Questions that Mom sometimes said would be better left unasked. "I'm hoping I can write a story about it for the school paper. You know, a feel-good people-helping-animals feature."

"Great idea, Ruby! People would love to read about this," Emelyn said as she tucked a strand of her straight black hair behind her ear. Her mom was a hairstylist and put temporary colors in Emelyn's hair all the time. Today Emelyn had bright blue streaks. The glittery green earrings she had on sparkled in the sun. Emelyn was the only one of us who had pierced ears, even though I begged my parents all the time to let me get mine pierced. Each one of her fingernails was painted a different color, so it looked as if she had a rainbow across her hands, and she wore a jean jacket that her mom had owned when she was a kid. If Ruby ever interviewed me, I'd totally go on record and say that Emelyn was the coolest person I knew.

"Yeah, maybe I can write an exposé. I'll call it 'The Secret World of Dogs' or 'What It's Really Like to Be Man's Best Friend.'" Ruby beamed, mighty proud of her titles. She always used big words. She was a walking dictionary. In fact, I wouldn't have been surprised if she read the dictionary for fun.

"What's an exposé?" I asked, because I most certainly didn't read the dictionary for fun.

"Like when you uncover a big secret," she said.

"What is it you're uncovering?" Emelyn asked, and Ruby let out a giant sigh.

"If I knew what I'd uncover, it wouldn't be an exposé," she said. "You never know what I could dig up. Maybe I'll show the world that you *can* teach an old dog new tricks, or what being 'sick as a dog' really means."

Before Emelyn could respond, a van pulled up and beeped its horn. Myka was the last to arrive, which wasn't a surprise. It would have been a surprise if she'd been on time. Her three older brothers were so busy with different activities that her parents raced from one thing to the next and called their minivan the family taxi.

Music blasted from the van's open windows, and her brothers waved and yelled dramatic goodbyes to her when she jumped out.

"We'll miss you so much!" Jordan yelled.

"Don't stay away too long!" Remy told her.

"I don't know how I'll function without you," Alex declared, his hand to his heart.

"I promise to write!" Myka yelled back before she ran over to us.

They acted like she was going away on an around-the-world trip instead of volunteering for a few hours. But that was Myka and her family. They were loud, loud, loud and always ready to celebrate anything, no matter how big or small. Seriously, I was over at their house once, and no one could get the lid off the jar of olives. When her brother Jordan finally unscrewed it, everyone cheered so loud, you'd have thought they were at the Super Bowl.

"Have no fear. I'm here!" Myka declared, and did a funny little dance that looked like one a football player would do when he scored a touchdown. Myka's motto could totally be "Go big or go home." When she was in the room, there was no mistaking that she was there.

She had on her soccer uniform, which wasn't a surprise. We joked that she was part chameleon. She took on the appearance of whatever sport she played. Last year she had walked around school for weeks in her karate uniform, this past summer she'd worn eye black even when she wasn't on the softball field, and I wouldn't have been surprised if she'd tried to wear her swimsuit during swim season.

"Let's go, team!" Myka said, and started a slow clap. "We're going to have a blast!"

"We might never want to leave," I agreed, and clapped with her.

"They'll have to drag us out!" Myka cheered.

The four of us headed toward the doors, but Mom playfully pulled me back.

"Remember," she reminded me. "You're not coming out with anything more than you're walking in with. In other words, no dogs."

I pretended to pout. "Not even if it's super-duper cute and fluffy and has a tail that wags fast when you look at it?"

"*Especially* not one that is super-duper cute and fluffy with a tail that wags fast when you look at it," Mom said.

"All right," I said, because simply being at the shelter made me feel like the luckiest girl in the world.

We entered a big room painted bright yellow, with a large desk against the back wall. The wall was covered with pictures of dogs, most posed

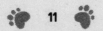

with smiling humans. A man with a head full of curly brown hair waved at us. He had on a hooded sweatshirt with the words MUST ♥ DOGS across the front.

"Hi. We're here to adopt a dog," I told him.

"Lauren!" Mom said, her eyes wide in disbelief.

I threw my head back and let out a giant belly laugh. There was nothing more fun than teasing Mom. "Kidding! We're your newest volunteers."

"Welcome aboard! I'm Mr. Turner, and I'm in charge of the volunteer program here," the man said. "Our dogs love meeting new people."

We introduced ourselves and gave him the permission forms our parents had filled out ahead of time.

"I bet you want to meet those dogs, so let me explain how this works. Most people think volunteering at a shelter is simply hanging out and playing with the dogs. But there is so much more work that goes into taking care of these animals. And while we love that you want to read to them, it also helps us out big-time when you do some of the other stuff too. So each week we'll have a task for you to complete, and then the reward is . . . reading to the dogs!"

"The cherry on top of the sundae!" Myka said.

"Sounds about right," Mr. Turner said, and chuckled. "Paws for Reading is a win for everyone. You get to practice your reading skills, and the dogs get to practice being around people. Some are very shy, and when the idea is to get adopted, hiding in the back of the cage doesn't help. We've found that our dogs who are read to interact more, which usually means they find a forever home quicker. And a forever home is our number one goal here."

The nervous feeling came back. Did I have what it took to help these dogs? I thought of Mom's words of encouragement and told myself yes, yes, I could. I could do this.

"Now to the task this week," Mr. Turner said. "We need the food and water bowls washed.

There's a sink in the back that you can use. Does that work?"

"We'd love to do that," I said, speaking for everyone.

Mom faked a shocked look. "Wow. I wish you'd get that enthusiastic when I ask you to wash our dinner dishes."

"I guess I've been saving my skills for here," I joked.

"I'll remember these so-called skills after dinner tonight," Mom said.

Mr. Turner took us through a door into a room that was lined with shelves of dog food. There was a huge metal sink filled with dirty bowls.

"The job is simple. Wash the bowls in one side of the sink, rinse them in the other, dry with the towels, and repeat."

"And repeat and repeat and repeat," Myka said, her eyes wide as she took in the giant tower of bowls.

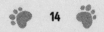

"There's a lot, but then again, we have a lot of dogs," Mr. Turner said.

"How many?" Ruby asked, always in reporter mode.

"Thirty-six right now. We're full to capacity, so every cage is taken."

"Thirty-six dogs without homes?" I said, and my heart hurt for each of them.

"Without *forever* homes," Mr. Turner corrected me. "By coming in to help out and read to the dogs, you're making their temporary home special too. We're glad you're willing to help."

"I wouldn't want to be anywhere else on a Saturday morning," I said. "Or a Sunday, Monday, Tuesday—"

"All right. I'll clean," Ruby interrupted, cutting me off before I could go through every day of the week. She took charge and gave us all jobs. "Myka, you can hand me the bowls. Lauren, you rinse, and Emelyn can dry. Does that work?"

"Aye, aye, captain!" Myka said, and saluted her.

"I'll help too," Mom said as she rolled up her sleeves. "No sense being here and not making myself useful."

We assembled into our positions and cleaned and cleaned and cleaned.

And then cleaned some more.

And cleaned even more!

It was like the stacks of bowls multiplied every few minutes. There seemed to be no end in sight.

"This is hard work," I said as I examined my fingers, which had wrinkled up like raisins from soaking in the water too long.

"Ruby, write that down in your notebook," Mom teased. "So Lauren can remember that the next time she asks for a dog. There's so much that goes into caring for a pet beyond simply playing with them."

And, wowsers, she wasn't kidding. It took more than an hour to wash the bowls, but finally, we were done.

Mr. Turner gave us the thumbs-up after we

asked him to come back and check on it all. "Great job! You're going to be a much-needed addition to our crew!"

"Does that mean it's time to meet the dogs?" I asked as the electric sizzle of excitement filled my body.

"You betcha," Mr. Turner said. "Did you each bring a book to read?"

I held up a copy of *Charlotte's Web*. It was my all-time favorite book. There was something so special about Charlotte. She was a tiny spider, but she made a huge difference in Wilbur's life.

"A good choice," Mr. Turner told me. "Okay, girls, when you head into the kennel area, grab one of the mats by the door to sit on. Find a dog you want to hang out with, and you can unlock its cage to sit next to them. We ask that when you read to the dogs, you do it in a soft voice and don't make any sudden movements that might startle them. If your dog doesn't come to the front of the cage, don't worry. It might take some time.

Remember, simply having you there is so great for them."

"And for us," I added.

"It's great all around," Mr. Turner said. "Now, without further ado, let's head into the kennel and meet the dogs!"

He opened a door, and when I stepped inside, I gasped.

HAVING LABRAD-OODLES OF FUN

"This is paradise!" I said as I spun around and took in the room.

Forget about white sand beaches, crystal clear water, and perfect sunsets. There's no place that could compare to a room full of dogs. This was true paradise.

We each grabbed a mat to sit on, and Mr. Turner motioned for us to walk farther into the room. "Go ahead and take a look, see who you

want to read to, and settle down and meet your new friend."

As we wandered past the cages, I wondered how you picked only one dog. I wanted to read to every one of them.

I stuck my hand into the cage of a tiny black puppy, who came over and gave me a bunch of licks.

"You're adorable!" I said. But he had a ton of energy, and I wasn't so sure he'd settle down for a book.

I walked past a few more cages, taking in the dogs. Each and every one of them was special, but I was on the hunt for the perfect dog.

And then I found him.

He was curled up in the back of his cage but lifted his head when I opened the door and stepped inside. He was medium-size with reddish-brown fur and gray around his snout.

"Hello, new friend," I softly said as I entered his cage. I held my hand out to him. He sniffed

 21

it but made no move to get up. So I backed up and gave him some space before I sat down. He watched me with his giant brown eyes. I held up my book and continued to speak in a low voice. "This one is my favorite. I hope you like it too."

I read the first chapter, and as I did, he slowly, slowly inched toward me until his warm body was pressed against my leg. I gently petted the top of his head, and he let out a sigh of pure happiness.

"I get it," I whispered. "I feel the same way."

My nerves from earlier evaporated and I got lost in the book. The time went by fast. Too fast. Suddenly we were being told to find a good stopping spot and say goodbye to the dogs.

"I'm glad I got to read to you," I whispered, and hugged him.

He licked my hand and thumped his tail a few times, which in my opinion was a dog's official way of saying "Thank you!"

"You have the magic touch!" Mr. Turner told me. "Rhett here is usually very shy and timid. He stays in the back of his cage most of the day."

"He's a sweetie," I said.

"He's also our oldest resident. He's been here longer than the other dogs. A little over a year. We love him, but we'd love it even more to see him get his forever home."

I bent down to pet Rhett and spoke directly to him. "Why wouldn't someone want a friend like you?"

"That's the age-old question," Mr. Turner said. "I wish we could figure out how to get our older dogs their forever homes. Everyone wants a puppy. People don't want older dogs. Puppies are cute, but they're a lot of work. Personally, I'm a fan of older dogs."

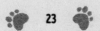

I thought about how lonely it must get when you live in a cage day in and day out. Did the dogs get to go outside? Did anyone play with them? Or did the older dogs spend their time watching the other dogs get adopted?

"I wouldn't mind an older dog either," I declared, bummed that I couldn't adopt one. I gave Rhett one more ear scratch before I left his cage.

"I wish everyone thought the same way," Mr. Turner said. He got a sad look on his face for a moment, but it disappeared as quickly as it had come. He swiped at the air with his hand as if brushing the thought away. "Enough of this gloomy talk. Will we see you back here next weekend?"

"Every weekend from now until I'm one hundred!" I promised.

"Perfect! I'll mark the next hundred years' worth of Saturdays down on my calendar," he said, and I loved the sound of that.

OLDER DOGS HAVE IT RUFF

It didn't take long for Rhett to become my dog BFF. I mean, how could anyone resist him? He was cute and cuddly and exactly the dog I'd get if I could have a dog. But alas, I wasn't able to, so I spent my weeks looking forward to the time I'd spend with Rhett. And from the way his tail wagged back and forth really fast whenever I showed up, I was pretty sure I was his bestie too.

Ruby, Myka, and Emelyn also had favorite dogs, but more often than not, they'd show up the next time and their dog would be gone, adopted by families. The younger dogs didn't stay long. Everyone wanted one. Rhett, on the other hand, was there waiting for me every Saturday, like a trusty friend you could depend on.

Week after week we'd complete whatever task Mr. Turner had for us—folding towels, untangling leashes, organizing the food and donations in the back room, or washing the endless stacks of dog bowls. And then, as soon as we were done, I'd rush straight to Rhett's cage to spend time with him.

On one warm and sunny day, Mr. Turner had us rinse and clean the kiddie pools that the staff used to wash the dogs.

"Maybe next week you can help give the dogs a bath. Just make sure you're not near Sampson when he shakes off," Mr. Turner said.

"We'd have to run for cover!" Myka said, and no one could argue with that. Sampson was a Great Dane and a true giant of a dog. We'd get a bath of our own if we were in his way when he shook.

"Speaking of towels . . ." Emelyn gestured toward her soaked cutoff overalls. When you have four best friends with a hose, sponges, and buckets of sudsy water, there's bound to be a water fight or two. "Can we grab a few in the storeroom before we read?"

"Of course, and then head on in to see the dogs. I'm sure by now you can find your way around this place by yourselves."

The four of us dried off the best we could and then rushed toward the kennel. However, when we got there, something was wrong.

Very wrong.

Horribly, terribly wrong.

I stopped so fast that Myka ran into me.

"Foul! Time-out!" she yelled, and rubbed her elbow, which had collided with my back.

"Where's Rhett?" I gestured to his empty cage as a bad feeling settled over me.

"Maybe he got adopted," Ruby said, as if your best dog friend in the world being adopted was no big deal. "I can see the headline now, 'Old Dog Finds New Home!'"

I should have celebrated with her, but instead it was as if a heavy rock had landed in my stomach. I chewed on my bottom lip. *This is great,* I told myself. *A home for Rhett is great.*

So why was I so sad?

"Wait? Did I hear Ruby right? Is Rhett in his forever home? Woo-hoo!" Myka cheered and pumped her fist in the air. I tried to hide my disappointment so that I didn't seem like an awful, selfish person. But I *was* a selfish, awful person, because instead of being happy, my heart broke.

"I didn't even get to say goodbye," I whispered. I was about to excuse myself to go to the bathroom, when I saw a familiar flash of reddish-brown fur enter the kennel area.

"Rhett!" I shouted. I ran to him and threw my

arms around him. His tail wagged in that familiar thump, thump, thump, and he nuzzled his head into my hand, his way of telling me he wanted his head scratched.

"Looks like Rhett knows a friend when he sees one," said Zoe, the staff member who had brought him in.

"He's my favorite," I told her in a quiet voice, so I wouldn't upset the other dogs.

"I totally get that," Zoe said, also in a whisper. "He's yours now. And with freshly clipped toenails. Why don't you take him back to his cage?"

She gave me the leash, but before I could go anywhere, Mr. Turner spoke up, "Wait a minute there. I have a better idea. Would you like to take him for a walk outside?"

"For real?" I asked, surprised.

"You already have the leash in your hand, and it's not like good old Rhett moves very fast," Mr. Turner said, and chuckled. "Usually we wait until you're a bit older to let you handle the dogs outside their cages, but you've proven that you've got what it takes. So what do you say? Are you interested?"

"Interested?!" I said. "There's nothing I would rather do right now!"

"Great! We have leashes in our utility room. How about each of you pick out one of the older dogs to walk?"

He didn't have to tell us twice.

I raced outside with Rhett, and the two of us began to explore around the shelter. I let him take his time to sniff anything and everything, and waited patiently when he found a particularly good scent in the grass. He loved it out there. And who wouldn't? The sun warmed my cheeks, and it was the perfect temperature, not too hot but not too cold.

"Looks like our buddy is having a great time," Mr. Turner said as he came up to me.

"We both are," I told him.

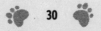

"This is where he belongs. We try to get Rhett out of his cage as often as possible, especially since he's been inside it for so long. It breaks my heart when I see how much he loves it outside."

"Mine too," I agreed.

My heart ached for Rhett in his tiny little home behind bars.

That did it. No more being relieved that Rhett was still at the shelter. He needed to get adopted. He deserved to be with someone who loved him and took him for walks every day, not just once in a while.

"Nope, not anymore," I said to Rhett. "I'm going to find you a forever home!"

"Talking to yourself?" Ruby asked as she came up beside me with a tiny little dog.

"Something like that," I told her. "Just think-ing about Rhett. I got upset when I thought he had been adopted, which I realize is stupid. He's been here way too long. It isn't fair; he's an amazing dog. I don't get why everyone wants a puppy."

"That's nonsense," she agreed. "The older dogs deserve a forever home as much as puppies."

"I wish we could help them in some way," I said.

"Maybe we could," Ruby said, and she called Myka and Emelyn over. She filled them in on what we had talked about.

"Wouldn't the shelter have figured out a way by now? Getting dogs adopted is their specialty," Emelyn said.

"Is that a challenge?" Myka asked, because Myka never backed down from a competition.

"A challenge I'm happy to be a part of," Ruby said. "Maybe we'll figure out the secret formula to getting these dogs adopted."

"Count me in too," I said.

"Who else is with Lauren and me?" Ruby asked.

"It's worth a shot!" Myka said as she pretended to dribble a basketball and then shoot.

"Emelyn, what about you?" I asked.

"Sure," she said, and shrugged. "Let's see what happens."

"That's more like it!" I said. If we could find homes for the older dogs, they would be able to enjoy the life they were meant to live. And that would be awesome.

However, there was just one problem.

How in the world *would* we find the older dogs homes?

4 YOU'RE BARKING UP THE WRONG TREE

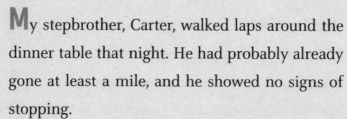

My stepbrother, Carter, walked laps around the dinner table that night. He had probably already gone at least a mile, and he showed no signs of stopping.

He called himself a professional walker. He said it was his full-time job, even though Mom and Scott reminded him that sixth grade was his job. Carter wore one of those fitness bracelets that counted your steps, and he checked it about a million times a day. He was in a weekly competition with his friends and took it very seriously.

When he bumped into the side of the table on a turn, Mom finally got fed up.

"Carter, we sit and eat together at the table," she said.

Carter gestured toward his empty plate. "I already ate, and technically I'm still at the table." Still, he plopped himself into his chair, but crossed his arms over his chest. He might have been doing what Mom said, but he wasn't happy about it.

I figured now was a good time to change the subject, before things went from bad to worse. I picked up my milk glass and tapped the side of it with my fork, the way people do at weddings when they want to make a toast. I then stood up on my chair to make my announcement.

Mom threw her arms up in the air. "Were my kids raised in a barn? Why can no one sit for dinner?"

Carter mooed like a cow, and I put my hand

over my mouth to stop from howling with laughter. Driving our parents nuts by acting silly was one of our favorite pastimes.

"You're going to hurt yourself, Lulu," Scott said, using his nickname for me. Scott claimed he was Switzerland, which meant he was neutral and didn't pick sides when Mom got upset with us.

I stepped off the chair onto the floor but didn't

sit. Instead I stood as tall as I could. I might be one of the shortest kids in my class, but I wasn't going to let that stop me. I wanted to look professional. Like I meant business.

"I have wonderful, life-changing news. News that will make you gasp and applaud," I said as I tried to add suspense. My teacher, Miss Taylor, had said that the best way to hook a reader is to use suspense. I figured that was the same with a live audience too.

"Oh boy. I can't wait to hear this," Carter said, and rubbed his hands together. "I hope you're going to announce that you're taking a vow of silence."

"Carter—" Mom started, but I cut her off.

"It's okay. He can tease me all he wants. Nothing can put me in a bad mood right now." I looked directly at Carter. "Not even my extremely annoying older brother."

"Don't keep us hanging. What's the news?" Scott asked.

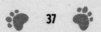

"The big news is . . ." I banged my palms on the table like a drum to draw out the drama. "Ruby, Myka, Emelyn, and I are going to save the older dogs at the shelter!"

I kind of expected everyone to burst into applause. My friends and I were doing an incredible thing. But my family didn't say anything. Well, until Carter spoke up.

"Um, what do they need saving from?" he asked.

"A sad, lonely life in a cage," I explained. "No one wants to adopt an older dog, so some of them spend months and months in cages. The one I read to has been there for an entire year. My friends and I plan to change that."

"That's great, honey," Mom said. "It's wonderful that you want to make a difference."

"A *ginormous* difference," I said.

"You've got such a kind heart, Lulu. I love that you care about the dogs," Scott said. I got warm and fuzzy inside from his compliment.

"Um, you're in third grade," Carter said.

"What's that supposed to mean?"

"How can a third grader change the world? That's like me declaring that I'm going to play in the NBA next week. Nope. Not going to happen."

"Maybe not for you, because you stink at basketball, but this is different."

"Yeah, right," he said. "You still sleep with a night-light and have Mom cut the crusts off your sandwiches. Do you really believe you can save the dogs?"

My stepbrother's words stung, especially since they were true. But I wasn't about to let him see that. I put my hands on my hips and tried to show him I was mighty, someone he couldn't mess with. "Just you wait. You'll be sorry you doubted me."

"I'll believe it when I see it," he said.

Ugh! Why did he have to be so annoying? Carter acted like he was so much smarter than me because he was three years older. Which, news flash . . . he wasn't any smarter.

I couldn't wait to show him that he was 100 percent wrong.

I *would* help those dogs.

I *would* find them homes.

DOG-GONE IT

"It's time to figure out how to get these dogs adopted!" Ruby said at school on Monday. She had a notebook open and a pencil, ready to jot down ideas. We were inside our classroom for recess because it was raining, so we had the chance to plot and plan.

Yep, that's right. I said *our* classroom! We were in the same class!

The four of us ending up together was like finding gold at the end of the rainbow or spotting

a unicorn in the wild. In other words, we'd gotten lucky times a million.

Our teacher, Miss Taylor, was the best ever. And not because she gave us snacks during silent reading, sang silly songs, and put emoji stickers on our papers. I loved all of that, but she was my favorite teacher because she didn't treat us like we were little kids.

"I might have an idea," I told my friends.

I pulled out a notebook of my own. I *had* been brainstorming and thought that I might have come up with the perfect solution. I pushed the notebook to the middle of the table, opened to a page where I had drawn stick figures and dogs. I had added arrows and crossed things out to help show my plan.

"Um, are we figuring out how to help the dogs, or doing math?" Myka asked.

I ignored her and pointed at my drawing. "So the shelter waits for people to come and find their perfect dog. And according to Mr. Turner, most people believe the perfect dog for them is a puppy. And who can blame them? Those cuddly little balls of fur catch everyone's attention with their extreme cuteness. The older dogs don't stand a chance. What we need to do is bring the older dogs to people. Match them up with their lifelong best friend. And *only* the older dogs."

Emelyn nodded. "That could work. It's not like we'll keep people from the puppies. It's just that we'll give the older ones a better shot to get noticed."

"Hmm . . . bringing the older dogs," Ruby said, and I waited to see what she thought. "I like it. It might work."

I smiled to myself. I didn't know if it was because of her reporting, but Ruby always seemed to consider the good, the bad, and the ugly of things better than the rest of us. If there was a problem, Ruby would find it. If she thought my plan was good, then it must have been.

I gestured for everyone to lean in closer. "I already have someone in mind," I whispered, and nodded toward Miss Taylor. "She totally needs a dog."

"Oh my gosh, you're so right!" Myka said.

"I can see it now," Emelyn said, and she got that far-off look in her eyes that she always had when she went into her imaginary world. "Miss Taylor and her dog sharing a big comfy chair by a fire. She'll grade papers, and he'll be snuggled up against her. There will be classical music on the radio and rain outside, but they won't care because they have each other to hang with."

She was right. I could totally picture it.

"Let's make it happen!" I jumped up and gestured for my friends to follow me to Miss Taylor's desk, where she was grading papers with a purple pen.

"Can we ask you a question?" I asked her.

She put her pen down and directed all of her attention toward us. "Of course. What's up?"

"We wondered if you live alone," Ruby asked, which Mom would have said was a personal

question, but Ruby always asked personal questions. She said that was part of being a journalist.

"I sure do," Miss Taylor said. That was another reason why we loved her. Even when we got nosy, she didn't seem to mind.

"Does it get lonely?" Ruby asked, another question that would no doubt qualify as personal.

"Not usually. I have my friends and family when I want company, and my awesome

 46

students to keep me busy during the day."

"But it might be nice to have someone around all the time," Myka piped up.

"Maybe," Miss Taylor responded. "But like I said, I'm content on my own."

Ruby wouldn't accept that answer. She continued her questioning with a different approach. "Well, say you did have a roommate. Would you want someone who has a lot of energy and always wants to be on the go? Or someone who would rather lie around on the couch and live a life of leisure?"

"A life of leisure?" Myka asked.

"Someone who likes to take it easy," Ruby told her. "You know, maxing and relaxing."

"Taking it easy is my speed," Miss Taylor said. "I like to watch movies or read."

"So someone to snuggle and cuddle with," I said.

Miss Taylor gave us a funny look.

"How do you feel about reddish-brown hair?

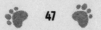

With a hint of gray? And brown eyes?" Ruby asked.

"And someone older and more mature?" I added, to make sure she understood what kind of dogs we meant. I didn't want her to think this was a good idea and then want a puppy. That was a mistake that I wouldn't let happen.

She studied us. "Girls, what exactly is going on here?"

We exchanged glances. Now was the time to seal the deal. To match our first dog with his forever home.

"We have someone we'd like you to meet," I said. "He is amazing!"

Miss Taylor gave us a surprised look. "What do you mean?"

"We need to find shelter dogs homes, and we have the perfect one for you," I explained.

Miss Taylor laughed. Hard. So much that tears formed in her eyes. She placed her hand over her heart and shook her head. "Oh my goodness. That's hilarious. I thought you were trying to find me a boyfriend."

Myka swatted the air with her hand as if a boyfriend were a silly thought. "This is a million times better than a boyfriend," she said. "His name is Rhett, and he's perfect for you."

"Yep, you two could snuggle on the couch together as you graded. . . ." Emelyn shared her vision with Miss Taylor. I had to admit, it sounded even better the second time around. Miss Taylor would be crazy not to want a dog.

"You four are too sweet," Miss Taylor said when Emelyn was done. "I'd love a dog, but unfortunately, my apartment complex doesn't allow pets."

"Why would you live in a place that doesn't allow pets?" Myka said.

"Yeah, that's the worst ever," I said, because I knew exactly what it was like not to be able to have a pet.

"Maybe you could move?" Ruby suggested.

"Wow, Rhett must be some dog," Miss Taylor said.

"He is, and there are a ton more dogs in the shelter who need homes," I said.

"It's admirable that you want to help, and I wish that I had a better answer for you," she said. "But I'm not able to have a dog."

"It's okay," I said, even though it wasn't. Not by a long shot. Because I was quickly learning that there was a big difference between *trying to help* and actually *helping*, and maybe Carter was right. Maybe we were too young to do big, important things.

A NOT-SO-FAR-FETCHED IDEA

There was only one thing that was guaranteed to make me feel better when I was in a gloomy mood. And that was a visit with Uncle Patrick.

I'm sure other people said they had the best uncle in the world, but they were 100 percent wrong.

No one was better than Uncle Patrick. He was a fellow pineapple-on-pizza fan, loved spontaneous dance parties, traveled the world with his husband, and brought me back the coolest souvenirs. But the best part was that he owned a cupcake shop! He specialized in mini cupcakes, so you could eat two or three at a time! (Or in my case, usually four or five. They were that good!) And his bakery was only a few blocks from our house.

Today I needed some cupcake therapy in the worst way ever. That was why, after we finished at the shelter, my friends and I went to visit Uncle Patrick at Sprinkle & Shine.

"I say this every time we come here, but I can totally imagine I'm sitting on a rainbow," Emelyn said, which was true. The shop was magical.

The walls were mint green with white stripes, and Uncle Patrick had painted the windowsills with gold glitter, so they sparkled in the sun. The tables were robin's-egg blue, and there was a different mini chandelier over each. A little flag with a heart printed on it was stuck in each cupcake, and all the cupcakes sat in a glass display case with twinkle lights. Behind the display case was a giant chalkboard that listed the week's flavors. Uncle Patrick sometimes even asked Emelyn to draw something on the board, which was impressive, since he also hired a grown-up artist.

"Not only is it the cutest place in the world, but it's also the most delicious!" I said.

"Speaking of delicious." Ruby pointed to Uncle Patrick, who was headed our way with a tray full of cupcakes, and glasses of lemonade with polka-dot straws in them. His red hair was styled into a high swoop like a wave, and he wore bright yellow glasses that matched his signature bow tie.

"My favorite girls!" he said. "I hope you came hungry. I'm counting on you to let me know which of these should be on the menu next week."

Yep, that's right. We were Uncle Patrick's official taste testers, and we took the job very seriously.

"You can count on us!" I gave him a thumbs-up.

"We always come hungry," Myka added.

 53

"What about you? Do you have any new ideas?" Uncle Patrick asked Ruby. Ruby loved to bake with her papa and shared her creations with Uncle Patrick. He had featured a few of them in the shop, and his customers were always huge fans.

"Not right now," she said. "I've been playing around with cheesecake and graham cracker crust. Maybe chocolate flakes on top. Basically I'm close to creating your next bestseller."

"You had me at 'cheesecake,'" Uncle Patrick said, and rubbed his stomach. He pointed to a pink cupcake with yellow frosting. "This is a bit different from cheesecake, but I'd love your opinion. It's pink lemonade. If you girls like it, I want to get it into the shop tomorrow."

I grabbed one and took a bite and then another and another until it was gone.

"Tomorrow won't work," I said, and I shook my head as I pretended to look serious. "I hate to break it to you, but . . . you need to put these out right now!"

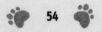

Uncle Patrick slapped his thigh in excitement. "Success! I thought the flavor was light and refreshing. Perfect for a picnic outside!"

"Speaking of being outside," I said. "We got to take the dogs for a walk! Volunteering at the shelter has been the best thing to ever happen to me."

"Wait, you? Enjoying spending time with dogs? What a surprise," Uncle Patrick joked.

"I want to take them all home," I confessed, which was when inspiration struck. "So . . . there are some sweet and lovable dogs there in need of homes."

Uncle Patrick began to shake his head. He could tell exactly what I was about to say. "I'd love a dog, but Uncle Imad and I travel too much. It wouldn't be fair to leave a dog alone so often."

"I guess you're right," I said, even though I was bummed to admit it. "We'll keep trying to figure out a solution."

"I hear that eating cupcakes is a great way to generate ideas." Uncle Patrick pointed to one with rainbow frosting and sprinkles. "Try those. They're for a little girl who is having a unicorn-themed party."

He didn't have to ask me twice. I bit into one, and it was like fireworks exploded in my mouth. Judging from the surprised looks on my friends' faces, the same thing was happening to them, too.

"What is going on?" I asked.

"It's a flavor explosion!" Myka said.

"Pop Rocks!" my uncle said. "I thought they added a little extra magic to the cupcake."

"I had no idea I could have this much fun eating a cupcake!" Ruby said, and grabbed another.

"Let's just say they're a blast!" Uncle Patrick said, and we groaned at his awful joke. "Okay, I've got to get back to work. Take your time testing the rest of them. This one is pumpkin spice, that one is caramel apple, and the green one is spinach."

We made disgusted faces. Spinach cupcakes?

"I'm kidding!" Uncle Patrick said. "It's mint chocolate chip. Let me know what you think of each of them and if you want any more. I aim to please when it comes to my VIP taste testers."

"Your uncle is the best," Myka said as he walked away whistling. "I can't believe we get to eat unlimited cupcakes."

"It's a tough job, but someone's got to do it," I said.

"The best part is when you discover a flavor combination you never would have tried but love," Ruby said.

"I wish we could get people to do the same and meet and greet all different shelter dogs," I said.

"A shelter dog taste test!" Myka suggested. It was meant to be silly, but it kind of made sense. "People could play with all different dogs, but especially the older dogs. They'll fall in love with them!"

"What if we did a tasting here?" I asked. "People could sample the cupcakes and meet the dogs!"

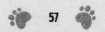

"You mean bring the dogs to the bakery?" Ruby asked.

"Yep! We lure people in with free cupcakes and then . . . bam! We introduce them to their new best friend!"

"Sprinkle & Shine would be the perfect place," Emelyn said. "We could do balloons and streamers, maybe decorate the cupcakes with a dog theme. And dog treats for our VIP guests, of course!"

"It's a fun idea," Ruby said. "But will it work?"

"Let's ask my uncle." I stood up and waved him back over.

"Ready for more already?" he asked when he got to the table.

"We're always ready for more," I said. "But this is about a brilliant idea we have. An idea that we need your help with."

The four of us explained our plan, and as we did, Uncle Patrick's smile grew bigger and bigger.

"That sounds spectacular! You know I'm always up for a party!" he said. "I'll donate the cupcakes and Sprinkle & Shine's patio if you can get everyone here."

"For real?" I asked.

"Of course! I'm happy to help a dog in need.

 59

Let me check my calendar, and we can pick a date. Then you can talk to the shelter and clear it with them."

I had been so focused on seeing if Uncle Patrick would let us use his bakery that I hadn't even thought that we would have to ask the shelter.

Would Mr. Turner agree to bring the dogs here?

Could he even do that?

Was our idea about to end before it had even begun?

TEAMWORK IS PAW-SOME

That afternoon I held Scott's phone and tried to work up the courage to call Mr. Turner.

Mom and Scott tried to give me a pep talk, but it turned into one big giant laugh fest.

"You can do it, Lulu!" Scott said. "I heard that you're so tough that when you cross the street, the cars have to look both ways!"

"She's so tough that she makes onions cry!" Mom added. "And before the boogeyman goes to bed, he checks under his bed for Lauren!"

"Wait, wait, I got a good one," Scott said, but he was laughing so hard that he had to stop to catch his breath. "Lulu is so smart that she counted to infinity . . . twice!"

I groaned. "Okay, okay, I get it. I can do this. I'll call Mr. Turner and ask him about our dog adoption event."

"You got this. You'll rock that call," Scott said.

I hoped I would. Because coming up with an idea was one thing. Now we had to make it happen. And Carter's words continued to linger in my brain and made me think that maybe I couldn't do this.

"Wish me luck," I said before any more doubts crept in. I dialed the number for the shelter and took a deep breath as the line rang. Scott pointed at me and then flexed his arms to show off his fake muscles. I tried not to crack up. He somehow always made things a little bit better.

"Hello. Erie County Animal Shelter. This is Karyn speaking. How can I help you?"

"May I please speak to Mr. Turner?" I asked. My voice shook, but I reminded myself I could do this.

"Just a moment," the woman said, and then I heard a familiar voice.

"This is Mr. Turner."

"Hi. This is Lauren. Your, uh, Saturday morning volunteer," I said. "My friends and I come in and—"

"Ah, Lauren . . . one of my hardest workers! I hope this call isn't to tell me you won't be able to help out anymore."

"Oh, no way," I said quickly. "I love helping out. I never want to stop."

"Phew! Good, because I still have you on the calendar for the next hundred years," Mr. Turner joked. "So to what do I owe the pleasure of this call?"

"Well, I, uh, I have a question to ask you." My tongue seemed too big for my mouth. I stumbled over my words.

I closed my eyes and pictured Mr. Turner at the front desk of the shelter, his wild hair escaping from under a hat, and the wall full of photos of adopted dogs behind him.

You've got this, I told myself.

"My friends and I want to create an adoption event for the older dogs. A way to get them more attention, since everyone likes the puppies best. My uncle owns the cupcake shop Sprinkle & Shine and said we could do it on the patio there. It won't cost you any money; he's happy to donate the space and food. All we need from you is to bring the dogs."

"I don't think I'll be able to do it—" Mr. Turner said, and my stomach dropped.

"That's okay—" I started, but he continued to talk.

"Nope. I definitely won't be able to do it . . . alone, that is! I'm going to need each and every one of our volunteers, since this is a great idea!"

he said. "We can very much help you make it happen!"

"Really?" I asked, nervous that this was a dream.

"For sure! We can talk about it when you come in next Saturday. Does that sound good?"

"That sounds great!" I said, and resisted the urge to cheer.

"And we'll make it our goal not to bring any of the dogs that come to the event back to the kennel," he said.

"That's our goal too," I told him, and thought about the cages full of dogs at the shelter. Hopefully, a lot of the cages would be empty before long. *If* we were able to pull this off.

8

A WORK OF ARF

My friends and I went into instant planning mode and spent the next week brainstorming how to make this the biggest and best adoption event ever. The pressure was on. It was up to us to bring everyone to the event. If people didn't come, the dogs wouldn't find homes. We had to get people's attention, which was why we appointed Emelyn to make the official event flyer.

"Prepare to be dazzled!" Myka said when we arrived at school that Wednesday morning.

66

"Emelyn has knocked this out of the park. She's created a masterpiece!"

Emelyn blushed. She was the most talented artist I knew, but she hated when people made a big deal about it. Mom said she was being humble, which meant Emelyn didn't show off her talents. But she totally could. Her art was that good.

Emelyn handed Ruby and me the most magnificent flyer. And I wasn't thinking that because she was my friend. It was perfect. Like it belonged on the wall of a museum, perfect.

She had written "Home Sweet Forever Home"

in bubble letters across the top and had listed the information about our cupcake/adoption event. At the bottom was a coupon good for one free cupcake and one free dog snuggle. It was brilliant marketing! Who could resist both of those?

"If this doesn't make someone want to help a dog, I don't know what will," I said, and Emelyn's face glowed with happiness.

"Thanks," she said. "It was fun to create."

"We should pass them out to the houses of people who don't have dogs. I bet Lauren knows where those are!" Myka said.

"Oh, I know every dog in this city," I bragged. "It's my special talent! I could definitely tell you what houses don't have a four-legged pal yet."

"Um, you forgot one important fact," Ruby said. "There's no way our parents will let us pass out flyers to strangers."

She was right. Mom didn't even let me ride my bike to the park by myself yet. I'd never be able to walk around our city and spread the word.

"That's a problem," Myka said.

"A big problem," I agreed, and Carter's words echoed in my mind.

I tried not to let his words bother me, but they did.

They bothered me a lot.

So much so that maybe it was time to tell my friends about what was going on.

"I didn't mention this before because everyone was so excited about our idea, but Carter acted like it was a huge joke when I told my family about our plan to help the dogs. He doesn't believe it'll happen because we're only in third grade. What if he's right?"

"*Only* in third grade?" Emelyn said. "We're awesome *because* we're in third grade."

"Yeah, Carter has no idea what he's talking about," Myka said. "He's being a typical obnoxious big brother. Trust me, I've had loads of experience with that. Besides, we have girl power on our side, and everyone knows that girl power is stronger than anything else in the universe."

"Okay, okay," I said before my friends launched a full-out revolution. "My parents are supportive about me wanting to help the dogs, so I could ask them to pass out some flyers for us."

"I bet my mom would pass them out at work, too," Myka said.

"What about Miss Taylor?" Emelyn asked. "I'm sure she'd help too."

"Let's ask," I said, excited that we had figured out a solution.

We quickly filled her in about the cupcake/adoption event, and from the way she nodded and grinned, it was obvious that she liked our idea.

"I knew you girls would come up with something great," she said.

"Emelyn made a flyer that will catch everyone's attention," Ruby said. "We were hoping you might pass some out for us."

"Of course!" she said. "I'll give the teachers a bunch and ask them to share with their students, families, and friends. It's the least I can do after I refused to move out of my apartment," she joked.

"Thank you so much. We appreciate it," Ruby said in her grown-up, professional voice.

"I'm happy to help. In fact, how about we start now and spread the word here?"

She rang the bell that sat on her desk. It was the signal for everyone to be quiet and listen. Twenty-one sets of eyes turned toward us.

My friends and I looked at each other, not sure what she had planned.

"I have an important question to ask everyone," she said. "How many of you like dogs?"

Everyone raised their hands, because come on, who didn't like dogs?

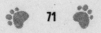

"And how many of you like cupcakes?"

All the hands shot back up, and Miss Taylor rubbed her palms together as if about to hatch a plan.

"Perfect, because I just learned about a special event that has both of those things! Girls, why don't you tell the class what you have planned?"

We filled everyone in on Home Sweet Forever Home, and as we did, our classmates whispered to each other, but not in a rude way. No, they were excited about it! So excited that Miss Taylor had to ring the bell again to get everyone to calm down.

"Okay, here's my last question," Miss Taylor said. "Who is going to come with me to meet some dogs and eat some cupcakes?"

And with that, our class went crazy. They cheered as if we had just found out we had a snow day.

"I guess that's a yes," Myka whispered, and

we cracked up. It was most definitely a yes.

Operation Forever Home was in business, and these dogs were sure to come out on top!

Nothing could go wrong now, right?

YELP FOR HELP

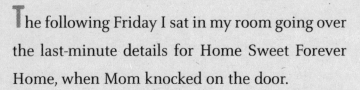

The following Friday I sat in my room going over the last-minute details for Home Sweet Forever Home, when Mom knocked on the door.

It was one day before the big day, and my best friends and I had worked nonstop to prepare. Scott printed a giant stack of flyers at work, and we'd passed out flyers to anyone and everyone we could. Emelyn's mom had told every client who came into her salon about the event. Ruby had written an article for the school newspaper.

And Myka had gotten her brothers to spread the word on their social media sites. The only task left was to go to Sprinkle & Shine tomorrow to help Uncle Patrick bake the cupcakes.

"I'm proud of how much time you've put into this," Mom said as she looked at the papers and lists I had spread out on my bed.

"It's the most important thing I've ever done in my life," I said. I waited for Mom to agree with me, but instead she sank down next to me.

"Honey, Uncle Patrick wants to talk to you," she said, and passed her phone to me.

"He probably wants to ask about what cupcake flavors we decided on," I said as I grabbed the phone from her. "This is Lauren, dog lover extraordinaire."

"Hi, honey," Uncle Patrick said, and I could immediately tell that something was up. He didn't have the happy sound in his voice that was part of what made Uncle Patrick my uncle Patrick. Mom joked that a tornado could pick up his house and take it away, and he'd still find the bright side. But today that was missing. In fact, he sounded exhausted.

"Are you okay?" I asked.

"I am," he said, and then let out a giant sigh. "But Sprinkle & Shine isn't."

"What do you mean? Did you run out of frosting? Use salt in the cupcakes instead of sugar?"

"I wish it were that simple," he said. "No, this is worse."

"Okay," I said, and tried not to let the panic reach my voice.

"Last night I ran the dishwasher before I left, which I've done a million times before," he said. "Except last night was the first time the dishwasher ever flooded. And when I say 'flood,' I mean a tidal wave of water. All over the shop. The floor has a few inches of water on it, and any of the boxes or supplies that were on the floor got soaked. We had to throw so much of our stuff out. It's a disaster zone."

"Is Sprinkle & Shine ruined?" I asked, and thought about how much I loved that place. I'd be crushed if he had to close the store forever.

"No, no, no," he said. "We'll be okay. I have a team in there right now to clean up. However, I'm short on supplies and there's no way I can bake in there for the next few days. I'm so sorry, Lauren. We'll have to reschedule the event for another weekend."

Reschedule the event? But what about the work we'd done to get the word out? And the planning we'd done? All our hard work had been washed away. Literally.

"I feel awful about it," Uncle Patrick continued. And I could tell by the disappointment in his voice that he did, so I couldn't very well get upset. It wouldn't be fair to him after all the nice stuff he'd done already to help us.

"If we don't have supplies, we can't have an event. I get it," I said, but just because it made sense didn't mean it was okay.

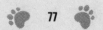

I hung up and thought about the flyers that were out in the community. How Miss Taylor had spread the word to her friends and family and how excited our class was. It was all anyone talked about. There was no way we could do this over again. Who would believe us? If we canceled once, they'd probably think we'd cancel again.

No, we couldn't reschedule, but without the cupcakes, we wouldn't have an adoption event. And without an adoption event, the older dogs might never get to know how incredible it was to curl up in their owner's bed or chase a ball in an open field.

Mom pulled me toward her and wrapped me in her arms. "I'm sorry. That wasn't the type of call anyone wants to get."

"It was a call no one should *ever* get," I agreed.

"Do you want me to let the other girls know?" she asked gently.

I wanted to say yes, but that wasn't the right thing to do. I had to be responsible, so I called Myka first to tell her the news.

"Sprinkle & Shine is closed?" she asked.

"For now. My uncle said there's a ton of cleanup they have to do, so we can't use their ovens," I told her.

"What about one of our houses? Could we bake there?"

"We could, but the supplies got ruined too. We need money to buy more."

"Maybe we could only have the dogs at the event," she suggested.

"Yeah, I thought about that. But people are expecting dogs *and* cupcakes. Otherwise, it's just like going to the shelter."

"I'll keep brainstorming," Myka said. "There's still time in this game, and I never give up until that final buzzer sounds."

"Thanks," I said, even though I was pretty sure that when time was up, we weren't going to end up being champions.

HOWL WE MAKE THIS HAPPEN

After I talked to each of my friends, all I wanted to do was crawl into my bed, pull the covers over my head, and fall into a deep, deep sleep.

Too bad sleep was impossible.

Carter had been right.

What had made us believe we could help the dogs?

My grumpy mood stayed with me all through the next day. I headed right back to my room right after school and dove back under the covers. I

 81

stayed there until the doorbell rang and there were shouts and laughter downstairs.

Laughter? Who would laugh at a time like this? I pulled my pillow over my head and tried to block out the noise.

There was a knock on my door, and Mom stuck her head in. "You have some guests downstairs."

"Tell them to go away," I grumbled. I wasn't in the mood to be polite.

Mom sat on the edge of my bed and rubbed her hand on my back in circles. "I know the news about Uncle Patrick is upsetting, but I promise that you'll like what you see downstairs."

I seriously doubted that, but I followed Mom to the kitchen.

"Surprise!" yelled my friends when I walked in. They were gathered around the table, with shopping bags, mixing bowls, and cupcake tins.

"What's going on?" I asked.

"You didn't think we were going to let those

dogs down, did you?" Ruby asked. "We're here to bake the cupcakes!"

"All the cupcakes?" I asked. How in the world could we bake the three hundred cupcakes we'd planned to have for the next day? And with what supplies?

"Every last one!" Myka said. "You don't know how hard it was to keep this a secret at school. I told Coach Soeder I needed to skip our game today, and she understood, so you're stuck with us all afternoon."

"And all night if we need to!" Ruby added.

"For real?" I asked.

"Would we joke about this?" Emelyn asked. "Saving dogs is a serious smatter."

"But the ingredients? They got destroyed," I said.

"My mom might have promised the owners of Hunter's Grocers free haircuts for life if they donated supplies," Emelyn said.

"Your mom is the best!" I said, and then I pointed. "And you three are the best of the best!"

"We are great, aren't we?" Myka joked. "Now put on an apron, grab a bowl, and let's bake!"

We became a cupcake-making assembly line. Ruby measured the ingredients, Myka mixed, I

scooped batter into the tins, and Emelyn kept watch on the oven. Mom even helped clean bowls when they got dirty. Once a batch came out of the oven, another one went right back in. The house smelled delicious, and cupcakes covered all surfaces.

At some point Myka turned on the radio. "Cupcake dance party!" she announced, and we sang and shimmied and twirled as we baked.

And baked.

And baked some more.

Three hundred cupcakes was a lot of cupcakes, even when you had the best of friends who'd shown up to help.

We continued to stir, pour, and bake as the sky darkened and my friends yawned. We were slowing down, and I wondered if we could pull this off.

"I don't know, everyone. It's almost seven, and we've still got a ton to make," I said.

Myka counted the cupcakes we had already baked and did some quick math. "We've done eight batches, which gives us one hundred and ninety-two cupcakes. That means we have five more batches left, to give us a little over three hundred. Easy peasy. We can do this!"

"Of course we can!" Ruby said, a streak of flour across her cheek. "Don't quit on us now, Lauren!"

"You think so?" I asked, because five more batches was still a lot when you could only fit twenty-four cupcakes at a time into the oven.

"I know so," Myka said. "If there were an Olympic medal for the perfect best friends team, we'd take gold."

"What good is girl power if you can't activate it?" Ruby asked, and then she turned to Emelyn. "Right, Em?"

"Oh yes," she said. "I'll be here until the sun comes up if I need to."

"So are you in, or are you in?" Myka asked me.

"Okay, okay, I'm in," I said as my doubts disappeared after my friends' explosion of girl power.

"I can't hear you," Myka said.

"I'm in!" I said a little louder.

"What was that?" Myka leaned toward me, her hand cupped around her ear.

"I'M IN!" I shouted, as loud as I could.

"That's more like it," she said. "Now let's finish these cupcakes!"

Myka's pep talk gave us the extra burst of energy to rally, and we continued to race the clock. The next morning would come before we knew it, but as we continued to work together, I thought that maybe, just maybe, we could make the impossible happen.

DON'T TERRIER
SELF UP WORRYING

I woke up the next morning still in my clothes from the day before, batter stuck to them, my hair dusted with flour, completely exhausted, and happy, happy, happy!

We had finished the cupcakes!

Every last one of them!

Hooray for teamwork!

They still needed to be frosted, but we planned to do that at Sprinkle & Shine, which, by the way, was now cleaned and ready to host an epic adoption party!

I took a quick shower and joined my parents and Carter outside as they packed the car.

"Today's the big day, Lulu," Scott said. "Are you ready for this?"

"As ready as I can be," I said, and a fluttery feeling filled my stomach. "But what if no one shows up?"

"*Everybody* will show up, and those dogs will be so happy," Scott said. "People want to support you."

I hoped he was right, because the dogs deserved it.

We loaded the rest of the cupcakes into the car, and Mom, Carter, and I pulled out of the driveway. I promised Scott that I'd tell him all about the event when we got home.

"Can you go slower? I'm afraid the cupcakes are going to get smooshed," I begged Mom as we headed toward Sprinkle & Shine.

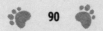

"I'm already driving below the speed limit. If I go any slower, we won't be moving. Relax. We're almost there."

Relax?

Do you know what it's like to drive with three hundred cupcakes in your car?

Three hundred cupcakes that took you hours and hours to make?

Three hundred cupcakes to help dogs who depended on you to free them from their life behind bars?

I'll let you in on a little secret. . . . It wasn't easy.

Every time Mom went over a bump, I worried the boxes would tip and the cupcakes would spill and crumble.

It was like someone had let a million grass-hoppers loose in my stomach. It was impossible to relax when so much depended on today.

We finally pulled up to the bakery, and before Mom could park, my friends raced out the front door.

"We have the frosting ready," Ruby reported. "Let's get those cupcakes inside!"

We had two hours before people arrived, and we would need every last second of it. Each of us grabbed a box and raced toward the bakery.

We soon found out that cupcakes and racing did not go together.

As if in slow motion, Emelyn slipped on the sidewalk and the box she held flew up into the air. It rained cupcakes everywhere!

"Oh no!" she cried.

"Are you okay?" I asked.

"I'm fine, but the cupcakes—" she said as tears filled her eyes.

I cut her off. "Don't worry. We have a ton more."

"A ton of *unfrosted* cupcakes," Ruby reminded us.

Myka helped Emelyn up and then put her fingers into her mouth and let out a loud, shrill whistle. "Let's go! The clock is running down and we don't have any time-outs left."

I rolled my eyes. Myka and her sports. But her words did get us back on track. Ruby cleaned up the mess, while we brought the rest of the cupcakes inside and got to work frosting them.

Uncle Patrick had a clock on the wall in the shape of a rainbow. I had always loved it until now. I could hear each second tick by and remind us we were one second closer to when everyone would arrive.

"We have to move faster," I said. We still had three boxes left to frost.

"I'm trying," Ruby said. And then she froze. "Whoops!"

"What happened?" I asked, terrified that another box had fallen to the ground.

She held up a finger full of frosting and stuck it into her mouth. "No worries. I've got this under control."

We worked as fast as we could, even as the

clock ticked, ticked, ticked each minute away.

"One more box left!" Myka announced.

"We're so close!" Ruby said as we moved faster and faster.

"I present to you, the last cupcake," Myka said as she passed it to me.

I added frosting and handed it to Emelyn. She had made the cutest little flags with paw prints on them and stuck one on top.

"Ten minutes until go time, and we're officially done!" Myka declared. "Let's get those dogs adopted!"

But before we could celebrate, Ruby spoke up. "Um, there's one tiny problem. We're missing an integral part of our plan."

"In third-grade language, please," Myka said.

"The number one thing we need," Ruby clarified.

"What's that?" I asked, and tried to think of what we might have forgotten.

"The dogs aren't here," she said.

HOME SWEET FUR-EVER HOME

Suddenly, as if the dogs had known we were talking about them, there was a bark from outside. And then another and another.

"They're here!" I yelled, and ran to the door. I bounced up and down like it was Christmas morning.

Mr. Turner was with a bunch of other volunteers from the shelter, and they all had dogs on leashes. Irresistible adoptable dogs with giant red bows around their necks.

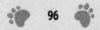

"We're so excited about today," he said. "And we can't express our thanks enough for what you girls have done for these dogs."

"They're worth it," Ruby told him as she bent down to pet a poodle.

"Yeah, I hope we can find homes for a bunch of them," I said.

"Or all of them!" Myka chimed in.

Mr. Turner chuckled. "I like the way you think."

"Come see what we've done!" I motioned for the group to follow me to the back patio. Some of Uncle Patrick's employees had set it up while we'd been frosting the cupcakes.

It was an adoption wonderland!

Music played from speakers, streamers had been woven through the fence, and balloons had been tied in bunches and placed all over. Pictures of the dogs were in frames on the tables, and there were bright-colored water bowls that matched the cups for lemonade. There were

tables full of adoption information and cupcakes. It might very well have been the best party I ever attended, and I crossed my fingers that everyone who showed up would feel the same.

"Success," Myka whispered to me, and gestured toward the volunteers, who gushed over all the stuff we had done.

Mom walked over and placed an arm around my shoulders and one around Myka's. "You did a wonderful job. How about we show it off to the people inside?"

"What people?" I asked.

She led me over to the door back into the shop, where a line of people waited. A *long* line. There had to have been at least twenty people already eager to come to our adoption event!

"They're here for us?" I asked out loud, and Mom nodded.

"And it seems as if they can't wait to meet some new friends. Are you ready?"

"You'd better believe it!" I said.

"Let's get these dogs adopted!" Myka cheered.

Mom opened the doors and waved the group outside to the patio.

Before long the space was packed with people of all ages. And dogs! So many dogs!

They wagged their tails, ran around, and got tons of ear scratches. Even the shy ones like Rhett were happily cuddled in someone's lap.

"You've got quite the crowd here," Uncle Patrick told us. "How about you say a few words?"

Emelyn turned to me. "You need to do the honors; this was your idea."

"This was *our* idea," I told my friends. "*We* made this happen."

I climbed onto a chair, and this time Mom didn't make me get down. Myka let out another one of her giant whistles, and everyone turned toward me. I should've been nervous, with all those eyes on me, but instead I was ready to show off our hard work.

"Thank you so much for coming today," I said. "We can't wait to introduce you to some of the greatest dogs we know. Trust me, you'll fall in love with every single one of them."

"It's true! You won't be able to decide who to adopt! You might even bring a few home!" Myka added, which got a laugh from the crowd.

"I could go on and on about how terrific these dogs are, but we won't make you wait any longer," I said. "So, ladies and gentlemen, kids and dogs, I hereby declare Home Sweet Forever Home officially started!"

The crowd applauded and I stood for a moment longer on the chair. I took it all in. Everything my friends and I had done.

"Remember when you were worried that no one would show up?" Mom playfully asked.

"Yeah, yeah, yeah," I said as I got down from the chair.

"You were a teeny bit wrong about that," she said, and winked.

"A teeny bit?" I asked, because no one could have predicted this turnout.

Carter came up to us and gestured around the patio. "Congratulations, Little Sis. You did it."

"Thanks! It's hard to believe that a *third grader* could make something like this happen," I said.

"What can I say? You proved me wrong."

I leaned closer to him and cupped my hand to my ear. "I'm sorry. Is there something the matter with my hearing? Did I hear you admit that you were wrong?"

"Believe it or not, I did," he said, and shook his index finger at me. "But don't expect it to happen again. You're still the most annoying person in the universe."

I made a face at him. Some things never change.

Mr. Turner walked over to us, his eyes wide. "I can hardly believe it, but we've found homes for eight of the eleven dogs, and a bunch of people have signed up to volunteer."

I thought my heart might burst from happiness.

"I've got to hand it to the four of you," he said. "You know how to get the important stuff done. You're special."

"Special for third graders," I said, glad that someone my age could make a difference.

"Special for *anyone*," Mr. Turner corrected me. "You girls are heroes to these dogs."

"Don't you mean '*sheroes*'?" I said, and I was positive that being a girl was the best superpower there was!

A PUP-TASTIC IDEA

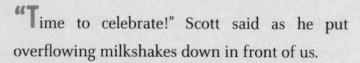

"Time to celebrate!" Scott said as he put overflowing milkshakes down in front of us.

Scott and I agreed that there was no better way to celebrate something big than with pizza and milkshakes. So that's what my friends and I did later that night. My parents let me have a sleepover, and the four of us talked about nothing but how wonderful the day had been.

"I propose a toast to a job well done," Ruby said. She raised her chocolate milkshake, which was more whipped cream than actual milkshake.

"Hear, hear!" Myka chimed in. Emelyn and I added our glasses, and we clinked them together.

"I can't believe we found homes for eight dogs," Emelyn said as she scooped her finger into the whipped cream on top of her milkshake and then licked it off.

"Including Rhett," I said. I'd thought I would be upset when he was adopted, but all I felt was happiness. How could I not? The older woman who was giving him a forever home had told me it was love at first sight, and the entire time she'd

waited in line to fill out his adoption papers, she'd continued to bend down to pet him, and Rhett would wag his tail each time! I had no doubt that the two of them would be the best of friends.

"When I interviewed Mr. Turner for the school paper, he said they don't usually have eight adoptions in one week, let alone one day," Ruby told us.

"It felt so good to find homes for those dogs," Emelyn said.

"What if this isn't the only great thing we do?" I asked. A little idea had wiggled its way into my thoughts on the ride home, and I was sure my friends would be as excited about it as I was.

"What do you mean?" Ruby asked.

"What if this is only the beginning? Think about it; we proved wrong everyone who doubted us. We did the impossible. Why stop now?"

"That's true," Myka said. "You never call a time-out during a game when the team is on fire."

"If we could find eight dogs homes in one day, imagine what else we could do!" I said.

"We would be unstoppable," Myka agreed, and bounced up and down in her seat.

"Exactly," I said. "Which is why we should start a club. A club where we do things to show people that you don't have to wait until you're older to make a difference."

"A club full of girl power!" Ruby said.

"Sign me up!" Myka said.

Emelyn raised her hand, the rings on her fingers sparkling in the light. "Count me in too! I'm all for changing the world."

"Let's do it!" I said, and my mind spun with the possibilities of everything we might do.

"What should we call ourselves?" Ruby asked. "Every club needs a name."

"What about the Remarkable Girls?" Myka asked.

"Or the Fantastic Four?" Emelyn offered.

I bit my bottom lip and thought about their

suggestions. "Those ideas sound good, but they're missing a certain wow factor. We need something that'll make people stop and notice."

"Something to make sure people never forget who we are," Myka agreed.

I thought back to earlier in the day when Mr. Turner had told us about the dogs who had been adopted. I had felt invincible. Like I could do anything. Like *we* could do anything.

"What if we called ourselves the Invincible Girls Club?" I suggested.

"The Invincible Girls Club," Ruby said, testing it out. "That's a cool name."

"I love the sound of it," Emelyn agreed.

"It reminds me of superheroes," Myka added. She jumped off her chair and did the Super-woman pose. "Don't mess with the Invincible Girls, because we're unstoppable!"

"So is that a yes?" I asked.

"A million times yes!" Myka said, while Ruby and Emelyn gave me the thumbs-up.

"Then I officially declare this the start of the Invincible Girls Club!" I exclaimed.

We grabbed each other's hands and squeezed. As we sat there connected, I thought about everything my friends and I had done and everything we would still do.

The Invincible Girls Club was here, and I couldn't wait to see how we would change the world next!

# Hello, Amazing Reader!

It's so nice to "meet" you! I hope you enjoyed reading this book as much as I enjoyed writing it.

Aren't Lauren, Myka, Ruby, and Emelyn incredible?

They proved to everyone that you can never be too young to make a difference.

Which is 100 percent true.

And guess what?

They aren't the only Invincible Girls.

They're part of a club that has been around for centuries.

Its members include Invincible Girls like Michelle Obama, Frida Kahlo, Amelia Earhart, Beyoncé, Ruth Bader Ginsburg, Susan B. Anthony, and Serena Williams. The list goes on and on. And the club is not only for famous people. No, not at all. It's also filled with Invincible Girls like you and me.

That's the coolest part!

We *all* have the potential to change the world.

We *all* have the ability to do great things, big and small.

We can *all* be invincible.

So let me extend an official invitation to you to join us, and let's show the world what the Invincible Girls Club can do!

Love,

Rachele Alpine

aka . . . a lifetime member of the Invincible Girls Club!

MEET
INVINCIBLE GIRL
Jane Goodall

Jane has worked with chimpanzees for nearly sixty years. When she was in her twenties, she went to Africa to study chimpanzees. She would sit very still in the jungle for more than twelve hours a day, watching how chimpanzees interacted. Eventually a group of them welcomed her into their family so that she was able to observe them up close! She saw incredible things, such as the fact that they live together in friendly groups, take care of each other, and even give hugs! Jane is an Invincible Girl because her love for chimpanzees inspired her to set up a foundation to protect them.

MEET
INVINCIBLE GIRL
Saengduean Lek Chailert

Saengduean was born in Thailand and spent her childhood helping her grandfather take care of sick animals. She fell in love with elephants when she was young. She was very upset about the cruel ways some people treated elephants, and she created two organizations; Elephant

Nature Park and Save the Elephants Foundation. She speaks out about elephant rights and has a sanctuary and rehabilitation center in Thailand for abused elephants. Saengduean believes in healing elephants with love and compassion, and spends a lot of time with them to show that kindness does exist. She's an Invincible Girl because she is working to teach the next generation of humans how important it is to live peacefully side by side with animals.

MEET
INVINCIBLE GIRL
Dian Fossey

Dian Fossey always loved gorillas and wanted nothing more than to keep them safe. She went to Africa and studied the endangered gorillas for two decades in the forests of Rwanda. Her discoveries were important and changed the way many viewed gorillas. She spoke about how they are peaceful and not aggressive at all, as many believed. Dian was an Invincible Girl because she campaigned against and worked to stop people from illegally killing gorillas.

MEET
INVINCIBLE GIRL
Dr. Leela Hazzah

Lions are amazing, and Leela wants everyone to know that! When Leela was a child growing up in Egypt, her father would tell her stories about how he used to be able to hear the roars of lions. She was sad that she couldn't hear these lions anymore because people had hunted and killed them, so they no longer existed in Egypt. She wanted to do something to prevent that from happening in other places, so she started a nonprofit organization that helps to protect lions in East Africa. Leela is an Invincible Girl because her organization not only helps keep the lions safe, but it also teaches people how important lions are.

MEET
INVINCIBLE GIRL
Bindi Irwin

Bindi has been surrounded by animals from the day she was born. Her father was Steve Irwin, the Crocodile Hunter, and his mission in life was to show people how spectacular animals are. Bindi has followed in his footsteps and speaks out about the importance of protecting our wildlife. She works with the Australia Zoo and the program Wildlife Warriors. Bindi believes that "we must be the change, seize the moment and speak for the voiceless." Bindi is an Invincible Girl because of her dedication, and her passion for animals and keeping them safe.

MEET
INVINCIBLE GIRL
Rachael Ray

Rachael Ray is a famous chef who has a lot in common with Lauren, Myka, Ruby, and Emelyn! She's made it a goal to help as many shelter animals as she can. She used her cooking skills to create a line of dog and cat food called Nutrish. The money earned from the sale of the food goes to the Rachael Ray Foundation, which helps animals in shelters until they can find their forever homes. She also believes that volunteering is important. She has said, "When it comes to giving, remember that your time and energy are just as valuable as your money." Rachael is an Invincible Girl because of her dedication to making sure all shelter animals are loved and taken care of.

MEET
INVINCIBLE GIRL
Seba Johnson

Seba Johnson has been a vegan since she was born. That means she doesn't eat or use anything that includes animal products. When she was young, she would join her parents to go to protests focused on animal rights. She is a vegan activist who has been featured in Black Vegans

Rock, a platform that gives black vegans a space to connect with and support other black vegans. Seba is the youngest Alpine skier to compete in the Olympics and the first black woman from the United States to ski in the Olympics. Despite her athletic feats, her dedication to animal welfare comes above her own successes. She was disqualified from a World Cup ski race because she refused to wear leather when she competed. She's also boycotted the Olympic games because of their host countries' unethical treatment of animals. Seba Johnson is an Invincible Girl because she uses her voice to support animal rights and other vegans who are on the same mission.

MEET
INVINCIBLE GIRL
Dr. Charu Chandrasekera

Dr. Charu Chandrasekera has a doctorate in biochemistry and molecular biology, and during her early career she participated in research using animals. However, she discovered that there was a lot wrong with testing on animals. After fourteen years of conducting research with animals, she changed her beliefs and practices. Not only that, but she works to change other doctors and scientists' beliefs about animal testing. Charu is an Invincible Girl because she is working to find alternative methods to research.

MEET
INVINCIBLE GIRL
Genesis Butler

Genesis is a true example that you can be an Invincible Girl at any age! She was only six when she made the choice to be vegan because of her love of animals. She started Genesis for Animals, a nonprofit organization that raises money to protect animals by providing homes and shelter for them. She was named PETA's Young Animal Activist of the year and gave a TED talk when she was ten! Genesis is an Invincible Girl for her mission to give animals new beginnings where they are protected and loved.

INVINCIBLE GIRL

Leah Garcés

Leah Garcés launched Compassion in World Farming USA, and she is the president of Mercy for Animals. These organizations care for animals and want to give them the best lives possible. Leah is unique because instead of working with animals who are hurt or mistreated, she has made it her mission to help animals before they are in need. She wants to prevent these problems. She has spoken out about the abuse of animals in the farming industry and travels the world to educate others about how to treat animals with respect. Leah Garcés is an Invincible Girl because she works to create more allies to make sure all animals are given humane care.

Ways That You Can Be an Invincible Girl and Help Shelter Dogs!

🐾 Adopt a dog in need of a home. (Or two or three dogs!)

🐾 Foster a dog until it finds its forever home.

🐾 Tell anyone and everyone how amazing older dogs are. (Because it's true, they most definitely are!)

🐾 Donate old bedsheets and towels to a shelter.

🐾 Take pictures of dogs who need homes and create posters about what makes the dogs so wonderful and lovable.

🐾 Make dog blankets out of fleece and give them to a shelter.

🐾 Make homemade dog biscuits and deliver them to a shelter.

🐾 Offer to go to a shelter and bathe the dogs or clean their cages.

 133

- Take pictures of the dogs at a shelter and share the photos with anyone and everyone you know, to get the word out about the dogs available for adoption.
- Walk the dogs at your local shelter.
- For your birthday party, instead of presents, ask your friends to bring an item that can be donated to a shelter.
- Help out with an adoption event.
- Plan your own adoption event.
- Take a book to the shelter and read to a dog. (I've heard that *Charlotte's Web* is a favorite of some dogs!)
- With the help of an adult, create a page on social media featuring dogs who are up for adoption in your area.
- Write articles for your school or local paper featuring shelter dogs up for adoption (especially the older ones).
- Learn more about some of the extraordinary organizations that help homeless animals, such

as Best Friends (bestfriends.org), the Humane Society of the United States (humanesociety.org), North Shore Animal League America (animalleague.org), Petfinder (petfinder.com), the Rachael Ray Foundation (rachaelrayfoundation.org), and Underdog Rescue (underdogrescuemn.com).

Acknowledgments

First, always and forever, thank you to the Invincible Girls in the world . . . past, present, and future.

Thank you for using your voices, abilities, and talents to make change, to stand up for those who can't, and to work to make this world a better place.

Thank you to the Invincible Girls who have not yet realized your potential and power.

Trust in yourself.

You WILL do great things.

Thank you to the Invincible Girls in my family, those who have helped shape and inspire me . . . my mom (Elaine), my grandma (Dorothy), my sister (Amanda), my aunts (Jeannine, Linda, Jan, and Karin), my cousins (Shelly, Tina, Carol, Joy, Jeannine, Barbara, and Michelle), my mother-in-law

(Beverly), my sisters-in-law (Heather, Amy, and Sirintip), and my nieces (Brooklyn, Addie, Ellie, and Maggie).

Thank you to my group of Invincible Girls, many of whom I have been friends with since I was young . . . Betsy Kahl, Jen Horn, Beth Moffat, Molly Nelson, Jenny Oliveira, Kelley Vlosich, Robyn Newman, Jeni Wamelink, Megan Simeon, Gina McGuinness, Jen Donovan, Becky Hoyt, Sarah Majeski, Roberta Kappa, Katie Kurtz, Lori Reigert, Lina Kosloski, and Kaitlyn Jonozzo.

Thank you to Elle LaMarca for being the greatest Writing Soul Sister in the world. You are such a strong, adventurous, courageous, and compassionate Invincible Girl. Thank you for the friendship and the conversations we have that cause me to think deeper and do better.

Thank you to my fellow teachers at Perry High School. I'm so lucky to be part of a group of Invincible Girls who day after day empower and inspire our students to be Invincible Girls themselves. I'm in awe of the work you do and the talents you share. A special thanks to Jodi Rzeszotarski, Jenny Hunter, Allison Trentanelli, Chris James, Rhonda Koch, Sonia Rodriguez, Deb Suba, Coleen Moskowitz, Lisa Gigante, Kelly Holderman, Rita Soeder, Pam Schlauch, Amy Sorine, Deana Scarano, Suzanne Tetonis, Jen Bezzeg, Michelle Carino, Lisa Hutson, Jen LaBoe, Heather Horton, Bonnie Kovacic, Terri Olix, Kali Borovic, Darci Murphy, Rachel Fier, Liz Shaw, Felicia Somogyi, Beth Singer, Denise Cogar, Brenda Elmore, Karen Kuhn, Sandy Lizewski, and Robin Parmertor, all of whom have worked tirelessly to show our students their worth, importance, and ability to become Invincible Girls!

The reverberations of two former colleagues still resonate throughout my school and my own life and choices. Thank you to Invincible Girls Cathy Priest and Kathy Traina. You have both challenged me to look at the world from different perspectives, question everything, use my voice for change, and stand up for what is just and for those who can't.

Thank you to my fellow writers who are Invincible Girls. Those who are telling stories about strong, passionate girls. Those who write about the tough stuff and celebrate the victories. Thank you for writing stories for all girls so they can see themselves and learn about others.

This book wouldn't be possible without the help of Invincible Girl Ella Soeder. Thank you for hanging out with my boys so that I could write (summer 2019) and revise (summer 2020). The two of them love you, and you're a great role model for them.

Thank you to the incredible group of Invincible Girls who worked on this book . . . Alyson Heller, Anna Parsons, Natalie Lakosil, Addy Rivera Sonda, Heather Palisi, and Alison Velea.

And a million thank-yous to my two boys, Harrison and Nolan. . . . May you always be surrounded by Invincible Girls.

 **140**

Turn the page for a sneak
peek at the next book!

THE INVINCIBLE GIRLS ✦ CLUB

THE INVINCIBLE GIRLS ✦ CLUB

ART WITH HEART

by RACHELE ALPINE
illustrated by ADDY RIVERA SONDA

ORANGE YOU GLAD YOU'RE NOT IN TROUBLE

"Emelyn," my teacher Miss Taylor said. "I need you to go to the office."

I froze, the tip of my pencil dangling over the math problem I'd been working on.

The office?

Okay, maybe I hadn't exactly been *working* on the math problems. I might have been doodling a picture of a cat, but that couldn't get me sent to the principal's office, right?

My classmates stopped what they were doing and turned toward me.

There was nothing worse than having the attention focused on you.

And right then everyone stared at me as if I were the most popular animal at the zoo.

I played with the cuff of my jean jacket and stared at the glittery nail polish I had put on the night before. What I didn't look at was my classmates.

"Ohhhhhhhhhh, Emelyn is in trouble," Nelson said in the most obnoxious voice in the world.

"Mind your own business!" my best friend Myka said. "She's not in trouble."

Myka was the most outspoken of the Invincible Girls, which was a club my three friends and I had started in order to make the world a better place. Right then I was grateful for Myka's support. With three brothers, she was a pro at standing up for herself. Myka didn't let anyone push her or her friends around.

I mouthed *Thank you* to her for silencing Nelson, because she was right. I wasn't in trouble.

At least, I didn't think I was.

Wouldn't you know if you were in trouble?

My brain switched into overdrive as I tried to come up with a reason, any reason, as to why I would be sent to the principal's office.

Sure, I was drawing during math, but I paid attention. I swear I did. Drawing helped me focus, and Miss Taylor had always been cool with that.

"Nelson, that's enough," Miss Taylor said, and she turned to me and held up an envelope. "I was hoping you'd run something to the office. It needs to get there now, and you're one of the most responsible students in the class."

She said that last part as she looked right at Nelson, who was nowhere close to the most responsible.

"So I'm not in trouble?" I asked.

Miss Taylor laughed. "Not at all. Quite the opposite."

It was as if the gray storm clouds whooshed away and the clear blue sky filled with rainbows, unicorns, and birds who chirped happy songs.

I was not in trouble!

I repeat, I was not in trouble!

"Thank you," Miss Taylor said as I took the envelope she held out to me. "I figured I could trust you."

"You sure can," I said, and heard someone snicker. I didn't stick around to find out if it was Nelson and his big mouth. I zipped out the door as Miss Taylor told the class once more to focus on their work.

The hallway was empty, which was weird.

The classroom doors were closed, and while I could hear the sound of voices, I couldn't make out any of the words.

Squeak, squeak, squeak.

The bottoms of my shoes rubbed against the shiny floor.

I glanced down at them and grinned.

It was silly to get excited about a pair of shoes,

but I loved mine so much. Mom had let me paint a white pair of sneakers we had found at the discount store. I made one hot pink and the other purple. I had added sequins and glitter and neon-green laces. They were the coolest shoes ever, especially since no one else in the entire universe had them. I was all about wearing one-of-a-kind creations. Myka called my style the nacho style.

"It's like the nachos my mom makes. She loads a little bit of this and a little bit of that and then a ton of cheese, and somehow they're perfect!" Myka had said to explain the name.

She was right. Today, along with my shoes, I had on cute, flowy, white wide-legged pants, a tank top with polka dots, and Mom's old jean jacket. My socks didn't match, but then again, I hardly ever bothered to match my socks. Who had time for that?

I did a twirl down the hall and imagined myself about to make my grand entrance at a ball.

A royal ball.

Yep, I was a princess headed to the fanciest party of the year.

This was my kingdom, and behind each door, people prepared to celebrate.

I closed my eyes and imagined the scene I would draw. A giant room full of windows and mirrors. Bright pieces of silk fabric would stretch across the ceiling, banners would hang from the walls, and candles would flicker on tables.

Mom said I had the best imagination of anyone she knew, and that was why my art was so incredible. I don't know about the incredible part, but I do love to draw. There is nothing more fun than picturing something in my head and then bringing it to life on paper.

Right then that picture was a far-off kingdom. I was so lost in this world that I didn't notice the wet spot on the floor in the world right in front of me.

Whoosh!

My foot slipped and I went flying.

I threw my arms up to catch my balance, which worked. But the envelope dropped and slid under the door to the janitor's closet.

"Great," I said to myself. "Now you really *are* going to get yourself in trouble."

I was reaching out to see if the door was unlocked, when the envelope shot back out from the little space between the bottom of the door and the floor.

Um, what?

I rubbed at my eyes.

Had I really seen that?

What in the world had just happened?

My mind flashed back to the castle scene I had imagined. Maybe there was a dragon hiding behind the door. I couldn't decide if that was cool or terrifying.

Or more likely there was a vent in the closet or some other boring explanation like that.

I inspected the envelope for dragon slime, but nothing looked out of the ordinary.

"Get your head back into reality, Emelyn," I said. I needed to deliver this envelope, so there was no time to hang around and figure out who or what was in the closet.

Suddenly there was a noise.

A sniffle-hiccup kind of noise.

A noise like someone crying.

And it came from the closet.

What should I do?

Miss Taylor had picked me to deliver this envelope, and there was no way I was going to let her down.

But someone was upset. I couldn't walk away, could I? What if something was wrong and the person needed help?

"You know what to do," I whispered. "You're an Invincible Girl."